✓ T5-CRO-142

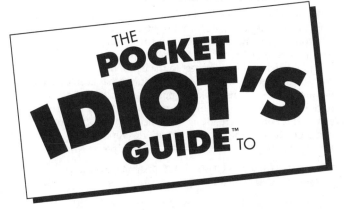

Living with a Cat

by Carolyn Janik and Ruth Rejnis

alpha
books

A Division of Macmillan General Reference
A Pearson Education Macmillan Company
1633 Broadway, New York, NY 10019-6785

THE POCKET IDIOT'S GUIDE TO & Design are registered trademarks of Macmillan USA

Macmillan General Reference books may be purchased for business or sales promotional use. For information please write: Special Markets Department, Macmillan Publishing USA, 1633 Broadway, New York, NY 10019.

International Standard Book Number: 1-58245-111-7
Library of Congress Catalog Card Number: 98-49276

01 00 99   8 7 6 5 4 3 2 1

Interpretation of the printing code: the rightmost number of the first series of numbers is the year of the book's printing; the rightmost number of the second series of numbers is the number of the book's printing. For example, a printing code of 99-1 shows that the first printing occurred in 1999.

Printed in the United States of America

Note: This publication contains the opinions and ideas of its authors. It is intended to provide helpful and informative material on the subject matter covered. It is sold with the understanding that the authors and publisher are not engaged in rendering professional services in the book. If the reader requires personal assistance or advice, a competent professional should be consulted.

Alpha Developmemt Team

Publisher
Kathy Nebenhaus

Editorial Director
Gary M. Krebs

Managing Editor
Bob Shuman

Marketing Brand Manager
Felice Primeau

Acquisitions Editor
Jessica Faust

Development Editors
Phil Kitchel
Amy Zavatto

Production Team

Development Editors
Beth Adelman
Dominique DeVito

Production Editor
Christina Van Camp

Copy Editor
Kristine Simmons

Cover Designer
Mike Freeland

Photo Editor
Richard H. Fox

Cartoonist
Judd Winick

Designer
Scott Cook
Amy Adams of DesignLab

Indexer
Tina Trettin

Layout/Proofreading
Marie Kristine Parial-Leonardo
Ellen Considine
Carrie Allen

Contents

Introduction

The earliest ancestors of the cat appeared on Earth about the same time as the earliest ancestors of humans—right after the disaster that killed off the dinosaurs. That was 65 million years ago. However, ancestors that we would recognize as having a family resemblance to the cats we live with today appeared about 10 million years ago. They were completely wild, and had no associations with the early humans. (Too bad for the humans.)

Archeological evidence suggests that some of these wild felines became tame and began to live in our company about 8,000 years ago, which isn't very long in geological time. (Just to give you a standard of comparison, it's estimated by some authorities that dogs have been keeping company with humans for almost 50,000 years.)

Since those first cats came in from the cold, the cat-human relationship has hit the extremes of love and hate. If one were to write the cat's version of the history of Western civilization, it would be packed with enough passion, hate, fear, and bloody gore to qualify for a prime-time TV series. Cats have been worshipped as gods and persecuted as devils. And they have survived.

Today, there are more than 57 million cats and more than 52 million dogs living in households in the United States, according to the Humane Society of the United States. A few years ago, cats passed dogs as the more common house pet—not that cats could ever be *common*, of course.

Within these pages, you will find lots of information about cats. That includes felines of all descriptions and in every situation possible, from breeds and how they evolved to kitty health care.

We hope you will find all that we have learned both informative and enjoyable. Good reading—preferably, of course, with a contented cat dozing on your lap.

Sugar and Spice

To add fun, extra facts, and new perspectives to the topics you'll be reading about, we've spotlighted items of interest by placing them in boxes. Here's what to expect:

Cat Language

There's a special language for talking about cats, and these boxes let you in on it.

Tabby Tips

You'll find tips on how to do things better, fix things, or get things. These boxes also contain warnings about products, practices, and situations that might harm a cat or its caregivers.

It's Been Said

From humor to inspiration, the words of famous people.

Chapter 1

Choosing a Cat

In This Chapter

➤ Points to consider for a first-time owner

➤ Shopping for your second or third or...

➤ Visiting a shelter—or having them come to you

➤ When you are looking for a purebred

You may be about to take the plunge and get your first fe-line. Or you could already have two or more cats, but you're keeping your eyes open for still another. Those new to this cat business will learn that owners often find it difficult to say "That's enough." The expression "Always room for one more" must have originated with cats!

You have many opportunities for finding your cat and plenty of places in your own community that, figuratively speaking (and sometimes literally), hang out the "Cats Here" sign. The experience that awaits you is likely to be curious, touching, funny, or incredible—maybe several of the above. However you hook up with your new pet, you will almost certainly have a story to tell about that match for the rest of your life.

Pop Quiz for Prospective Owners

Are you about to look for your very first cat? Let's go over your thinking about that move.

Why do you want a cat? That seems obvious, of course. You want the companionship of a pet around your place. You look forward to the amusement its antics will provide. There is a vacancy in your life for a pet, and a cat is what will fill the bill. Maybe you want a pet in order to introduce your children to animals and to the responsibility of caring for them.

On the other hand, perhaps you are Ernie of Ernie's Deli, and you are looking for a cat to keep down the rodent population at the restaurant. That's a valid reason for cat shopping too, as long as you will care for that animal.

Whatever your reason for wanting a cat now, here is an important point to consider: These days, a cat's life span can be 15 or 20 years or even longer. Be certain you are ready to make that lengthy commitment.

Is your life reasonably stable? If you are leaving for college in a few months, moving to England, or about to get a divorce, you might want to put taking in a pet on the back burner until things settle down.

Do you have the time to devote to a pet? The cat chosen for work in a store or other setting will find its days full—or its nights if it is working the graveyard shift. But the cat that is brought into a house or apartment as the sole pet has different needs. If you leave for work at 8:00 A.M., return home at 6:30 P.M., eat dinner, watch some television, and are in bed by 11:00 to sleep until 6:30 the following morning, pussy is virtually alone more than 20 hours a day, because your sleeping time is not exactly stimulation for your cat. If you travel frequently in your job, that is worse yet.

It is not kind to take a pet for the enjoyment it can bring you if you cannot offer it some fun in return. In a two-person household where one of you does not work outside the home, the cat may receive plenty of attention. The same applies to a working household where everyone's hours are staggered.

If your cat is going to be alone a huge chunk of the day, there are ways you can keep it happy. You can also try to choose a shy or calm cat who, while certainly friendly, can manage solitude better than the "high maintenance" pet who needs a good deal of its owner's attention.

Another option is to take two cats. They can play with each other, and just knowing another animal is in the home can make a feline more content. Two cats are no more work than one, but are, of course, more expensive.

Can you afford the cost of cat ownership? Food is a running tab, of course, but there is also cat litter, some toys, regular veterinarian checkups, and perhaps a major vet bill some day for a serious illness or an accident. There might be occasional boarding or pet-sitting fees. Will you be able to manage all of that?

Pet ownership is not a formidable expense—except for that major illness tab—but it does call for an ongoing outlay of cash.

This brief quiz no doubt set you thinking about the very real changes a pet will bring into your home and how responsible you will be for that little life. You probably passed with flying colors. Here are just a few more points to consider before you go shopping.

Do You Already Have a Cat or Two or...?

Perhaps your dowager 21-year-old cat has recently died. Although you have two younger pets, you are naturally missing your companion for its own special personality and you also notice the void its loss brings. Pretty soon, while still mourning Smudge, your thoughts turn to another cat. Not a replacement, of course. There was—and will be—only one Smudge. But the new cat will be a replacement in the sense that it will bring your cat complement back up to three. A comfortable number, you feel.

Just be certain that when you go cat shopping you will have the heart to appreciate your new cat for it's own uniqueness.

Maybe death is not the reason why you are looking for cat number three (or number four). Perhaps you just plain want another cat. Well, why not? There's no quota system here, but only practical considerations, such as whether your town, landlord, or homeowners association will allow as many cats in your household as you would like; whether you have space for another pet; and whether you can financially care for one more. Oh, and maybe one other thing: Will your current cat(s) accept the newcomer? (There are some suggestions for introducing a new pet to the others in Chapter 4.)

Kitten or Adult, Male or Female?

Decisions, decisions. Who can resist the antics of a kitten, a tiny ball of fluff whose face seems to be almost entirely wide, bright eyes? Not many. If you opt for a kitten, you are indeed getting moments that will make you laugh out loud as it explores your home and life in general. You can also look forward to what is likely to be a long life for your pet.

But that kitten will grow to be an adult cat. Also, kittens are fragile and subject to illness and injury. Maybe all that kittenish activity will be a little too much for you, too. If so, consider the grown-up cat. "Grown-up" can be as youthful as one or two years old, or just plain old (starting at around 10). For adoption purposes, the adult cat can be as young as 9 or 10 months, just past that cute kitteny stage.

The advantages of an older cat are:

➤ You can determine its temperament now instead of waiting for it to mature, making your selection a little easier.

➤ It has passed through the illnesses of kittenhood.

➤ You are spared the sometimes hyperactivity of kittens.

➤ It may have been spayed or neutered.

Do not think older cats are not fun. They will make you laugh too, with their own special quirks and sometimes outrageous behavior.

The older cat might have some already apparent health problems, and others might crop up sooner than they would with a younger cat. Some mature cats have been neglected or mistreated in the past and may need time to settle into their new homes. However, many more oldsters have been given up because of an owner's allergies, a move, or similar circumstances not related to behavior. And, of course, the older the cat, the fewer the years you will have left with your pet.

Which is better? It's your call. Felines of all ages need loving homes.

As to whether your cat should be male or female, that too is up to you. Altered males and females, those that have been neutered or spayed, both make good house pets.

Some say you cannot tell the difference in temperament between the two.

One more decision to make here: a longhaired or short-haired pet. If you opt for the former, remember that the animal must be frequently groomed, more so than a shorthaired cat.

Of Course Cats and Dogs Can Live Together

Where did the phrase "They fight like cats and dogs" come from? Letting a new cat join your Irish Setter, or perhaps the setter and your spaniel, can often work out well. See Chapter 4 for introducing everyone to one another and attempting to have harmony reign.

Your Local Animal Shelter

Many towns have an animal shelter, and big cities usually have a few, operated by a variety of sponsoring organizations. Virtually all do a sterling job of trying to find homes for animals that have been lost or discarded. Almost all experience a constant financial crunch, too.

You can almost always find a cat you want in a shelter, even a purebred, although they do not find their way into those facilities in the same numbers as the more ordinary "household" cats.

By getting your pet from a shelter, you are saving the life of an animal who might have no future at all. Don't worry about the cat you find in this manner. Good shelters screen out animals with serious behavior problems.

Rules and regulations for adoption vary from one place to another, and some screening usually takes place. For example, if you are under 18 years of age, you will probably have to secure the signed consent of a parent or guardian for the adoption. Perhaps the shelter you are visiting does not allow adoptions during the Christmas season, or indeed adoptions of pets as gifts for others at any time of the year. They fear for the well-being of animals adopted for friends or relatives of those visiting the shelter, gift recipients who might not *want* those cats.

Tabby Tips

If you want to give a cat from a shelter as a gift, wrap up a cat toy to present to the recipient with a note saying that the kitten or cat is to follow. Some shelters offer gift certificates or cards that you can give along with the toy.

You can usually expect to give a donation of anywhere from $10 to $100 for your pet, which might include spaying or neutering and/or some vaccinations. It's wise to call a shelter first to find out what you need to bring with you.

Look around the shelter you visit. Is it clean? Are the cages clean? Is the staff pleasant and helpful?

Take your time looking at the cats. Perhaps you are sure you want a black kitten, but do allow yourself to become acquainted with some of the others. Maybe a paw will reach out to you through the bars, and the cat you take home will be gray and white, and not at all little. If you see two adult cats in one cage, obviously getting along well, they could be littermates or cats raised in the same household. Give some thought to taking both. It would be a shame to separate good buddies, and, as mentioned earlier in this chapter, having two cats can be a good move for both owner and pet.

Tabby Tips

Sometimes cats will come to you. Many animal shelters bring "petmobiles" to shopping malls, citywide community events, and other places where there are a large number of possibilities for pet adoption. From time to time, a shelter will tote a few cages of cats and dogs to the lobby of a major office building.

Ask a member of the staff about any cat that interests you. Some details will be on a card attached to that animal's cage, such as the pet's medical history, if it is known, and its present state of health. The staff can usually provide more information based on daily contact. Has that cat been friendly? Shy? Aggressive? What type of temperament do you prefer in your pet? Are there certain personality traits and health problems that go along with that breed? If you can, it is wise to bring every member of the household with you before choosing a specific cat. Some cats could be frightened of children. Some may not like men, others back away from women.

If for some reason the cat does not work out, despite everyone's best intentions, you can return it. Good shelters will take pets back so they will have another chance at a happy home.

Answering Advertisements

"Wanted," the newspaper or bulletin board advertisement reads, "Good homes for five playful, gray, eight-week-old kittens, two males, three females. Call 555-1212."

This is another path to adoption that can work out very well. Cats born in a home, usually of house cats, are already in a good environment and are comfortable around people.

If you have never seen a new litter of kittens before, prepare to spend some time just going "Awwww." They will be cute. They will be *adorable*.

When you can finally get down to business, notice the cat mom and her temperament. Ask the homeowners about it, too. Is the litter from a house cat, or was it found outdoors? Have they been to a veterinarian? Look closely at the kittens (as if you can take your eyes away from them). Does one seem to be the leader? Is one very shy? Which is the runt, or smallest of the litter? Have they been litter-box trained? See Chapter 3 for an additional checklist of points to note.

It is wise not to take a kitten younger than six or eight weeks from its mother. It is learning much from mom, and that attachment, plus its socialization with littermates, will bode well for its life ahead.

Unless it is pedigreed, the cat you find through an ad is usually, but not always, free.

Finding a Cat at the Vet's

Many veterinarians go beyond treating cats and also help to find homes for them. Most vets let people place notices of available cats on a bulletin board, but some also keep a few strays in the office, just waiting for adoption.

There are advantages to finding your cat through a vet's office. Obviously, it is people who care and are knowledgeable about cats, probably owning one or a few, who place the notices on the bulletin board and bring in pets who need homes. The vet has probably checked out the animals, as well.

You can stop in at a veterinary clinic to look around, even if you have never had a pet or you have none at the moment. Just one thing: Don't try to adopt office cats or mascots. The staff will not let anyone have the cuties that perch on their computers, doze on the file cabinets, and officially greet visitors!

On the Trail of a Pedigreed Cat

When you know exactly what type of cat you want, and it is not the typical mixed breed that fills the shelters (although a few pedigreed cats do find their way there), you will want to visit a breeder. You are shopping for a Turkish Angora, for example, or a Scottish Fold.

These animals are bred from a known pedigree lineage to conform to a written standard that describes what, ideally, that breed should look like. Pedigreed cats are not common in this country, comprising only about 5 percent of the feline population.

It is wise to decide before heading for a breeder whether you want a house pet or a cat to show at organized cat shows. If it's a show cat, try to attend some meetings of a local cat club before definitely electing to enter that arena. Showing cats requires work and money.

Breeders know about genetics, temperament, and overall care for the breed, or two or three breeds, that they raise. Some men and women in this field have made remarkable contributions to knowledge about the breed that they specialize in.

You can pay from $100 to several thousand for a pedigreed cat, depending on the breed you want and your geographical location. For the "papers" part of this transaction, you should get a pedigree certificate with the animal's family tree, a transfer certificate that shows you now own the cat, and immunization documents.

Cat Language

A **cattery** is a place where pedigreed cats are raised to be sold as pets, for breeding or for show.

By all means, shop around from one breeder to another the way you would shop for any purchase. You can find breeders by checking advertisements at the back of cat magazines, by attending a regional cat show, or by contacting cat breeding registries.

The Pet Shop Cat

How much is that kitty in the window? Usually quite a bit. This is the expensive way to find a pet because you are paying a middleman—the pet store owner.

Kittens, not full-grown cats, are the specialty in pet shops because they are so irresistible to potential buyers. Many will be purebreds. The problem here, of course, is the background of pet shop kittens. Many are bred indiscriminately (yes, there are kitten mills the same way there are puppy mills), where the emphasis is less on the care of the animals than on future profits. Also, the kittens are subject to disease, certainly stress, and are not used to the love and attention so critical in the early days and weeks of a cat's life.

If you see a kitten you fall in love with at a pet shop and truly want to buy that cat, look around to be sure the store is clean, the animals look healthy (see Chapter 3), and the store owner seems conscientious. Talk to him or her and try to determine as much of the history of that kitten as possible.

Some pedigreed cats wind up in pet stores because they do not conform 100 percent to the standard for that breed. They will not make good show cats, if that is your intention. Ask about "papers" and what the store is ensuring about vaccinations and health-related guarantees. The minimum you should accept is a 14-day guarantee with a full refund. Better yet is one for 30 days against congenital defects, which could be slow to appear.

Some states have a pet "lemon law" requiring that any dog or cat offered for sale be accompanied by an official certificate of veterinary inspection. The certificate lists all vaccines and deworming medications administered to the animal and states that the examining vet warrants that, to the best of his or her knowledge, the cat or dog has no sign of contagious or external parasites. Check with your community's Department of Consumer Affairs to see if such a law, or one similar, is in effect where you live.

It's Been Said

"There are two means of refuge from the miseries of life: music and cats."

—Albert Schweitzer

Chapter 2

When a Cat Chooses You

In This Chapter

➤ The many ways of coming across a cat

➤ The differences among strays

➤ It takes skill to handle a scared cat

➤ Finding a home for the homeless—your place, maybe?

More than one cat owner has come by his or her pet accidentally, almost literally stumbling over that patch of fur. Sometimes the cat or kitten appears around the prospective owner's home, insinuating itself so cleverly into that home life that it finally becomes adopted.

They are everywhere, these lost kittens or adult cats, looking for shelter and a good home. Some day one could bring itself to your attention and make you a rather surprised first-time cat owner. Or, if you have a cat or two at home, you might invite one of these orphans to join your brood.

The Stray, Sort of

One summer, two of four Virginia house cats became parents of a litter of three kittens. Perhaps because there was some renovation work going on in the house at the time and there were three other cats and dogs there, the mother cat seemed to want some peace and quiet for a while. After a few weeks she led her kittens across the street, where they took up residence on a neighbor's front porch. The neighbor fed the mother cat and, after they were weaned, the kittens.

Eventually one kitten, all by itself, toddled back to its original house. This cat wanted to be where the action was, and it also wanted to be petted—a lot. The owner welcomed it back and easily found it a wonderful home where, now named Mopsy, it was the center of it's people's—and the other house cats'—attention.

Lesson: Some cats, like some people, go after a better life instead of waiting for it to come to them.

The Virginia cat was not a stray, even though it showed up on that owner's doorstep. But some day *you* could hear a plaintive mewing that comes attached to a cat that looks scraggly, or even to a cat that looks fine and fed. The cat can be on your front porch, at your back door, or in your basement. For some folks, a mysterious caller comes into their home through an open window and presents itself on the kitchen counter or the mantel. Voilà! There is a cat from...well, who knows? It seems to want to stay, though.

Maybe you will meet your stray away from home. You might come upon a litter in a city alley or in the woods near your neighborhood. Or you might find a litter of very small kittens in the supermarket parking lot.

It should be said here that there are indoor cats, and there are those who live outdoors but are fed by neighbors. The latter might be tame, but often they are what is known as feral, or wild, cats. It is usually, although not always, too late to bring them into one's home and expect them to settle down and become serene house pets.

Of course, it is not the feral cat that is going to plead to be allowed inside your home, although there are always exceptions. When they become ill or old—or just a little more mellow—a few feral cats allow themselves to be coaxed into the home of the person who has been feeding them. But generally, however, they are not interested in the domestic life, coming within a certain distance of the house only at mealtimes.

You might have a chance of finding good homes for the feral cat's *kittens,* if you can get to them early enough (if the cat allows you near them). It is also good for the always-burgeoning cat population to bring the feral cat to the vet for spaying or neutering. There is some information on how to catch those elusive felines later in this chapter.

Cat Language

Spaying is the procedure that removes the reproductive organs of female cats and dogs. Male dogs and cats are **neutered** by removing both testicles. Your vet can explain these procedures to you and advise the best age for sterilization.

Here is a point to note in the rescuing-strays business: More than one kindhearted soul, new to saving cats, has reasoned, "I'll bring it home, put it in the yard, and give it a good meal. Then it will be able to travel through the neighborhood and someone will adopt it."

Uh-uh. Feed it once, and it will probably consider itself yours, unless you pick it up and deliver it somewhere else. Naming a stray also usually spells doom for your plans to find a home for the fuzzball. In both instances, congratulations are probably in order on the new addition to your household.

Handling the Frightened Cat

Who wouldn't be frightened far from what might have once been a warm home, hungry, scared of one's surroundings, and, in some cases, concerned about a litter of even more helpless kittens?

Rescuing an adult cat, or perhaps a mother cat and her litter, will take some careful planning, whether they are found in the bushes behind your home or in a supermarket lot. Normally placid animals can snap and bite under duress or, worse for your purposes, flee and become impossible to catch.

Whether you are catching a cat for your own home, to place for adoption, or to turn over to a shelter, give some thought to this process before setting out.

If you have no cats at home, you will want to be prepared for your stray with cat food, litter, a water bowl, and perhaps bandages if the animal seems wounded.

Tabby Tips

A local animal shelter might have more sophisticated tools that they lend or rent to help catch strays. These might include a cat net, a "cat grabber" (a pole-like gadget with tongs), or a humane cat trap.

You will need a pet carrier or cage, or at least some large towels in which to wrap the cat. A pair of gardener's gloves or leather gloves will help save your hands from scratches and bites, but will not offer total protection.

Call quietly to the cat so as not to scare it even more. A sort of "Here kitty, kitty, kitty" will do, plus other bits of conversation that, you hope, will put it at ease. When you actually catch it, the cat could be docile, but it is wise to prepare for hisses, scratches, and, perhaps, bites. Brace yourself for the worst so that you are not surprised and do not lose the animal.

What we are talking about here is the—at first glance— healthy cat that does not seem feral. The cat that is obviously very sick will call for a different strategy. If it is staggering and having convulsions, it could have rabies. If you see a discharge from its eyes and nose, the cat might be suffering from an upper-respiratory infection or even feline distemper.

If You Find a Stray Cat

- ➤ Keep it separate from other pets in your home.

- ➤ Look for identification so that you can return it to its owner.

- ➤ If there is no identification, call area shelters and your local pet control office to see if anyone is looking for that animal.

- ➤ If there is no response from the owner, discuss keeping the pet with other members of the household.

- ➤ If keeping it is not possible, try to find a home for the cat.

- ➤ Still no luck? Take it to a shelter, perhaps one that allows cats to live out their lives there.

You will have to choose between trying to rescue this cat yourself or calling for assistance. If the cat goes to a shelter, you must decide whether to pay for its treatment and try to find a home for it, perhaps with you.

A Litter of Very Young Kittens

Step near a litter with the mother cat in attendance and you can expect some fuss from her. If you manage to rescue them all and the mom is still nursing the kittens, you will not have to worry about food for your young strays, at least for the moment. It's when you find a kitten or an entire litter all alone that you will have to see to their meals.

Keep Everyone Separated for a While

It is wise to keep any homeless cat or kitten separate from your brood until you know the state of its health. You don't want it passing contagious diseases or parasites to your pets. There is more about having a vet look at a "new" cat in the next chapter.

You can put your stray in the basement (if it is winter and the space is warm), in a tool shed, or in an extra room or bathroom in the house. The cat will be quite comfortable with food and water bowls, a litter box (not too close to the food), a bed you have fashioned for it, perhaps a few toys, and, of course, you coming to visit often.

Finding a Home for the Homeless

When the stray(s) you have found, or the one that has found you, has settled down a bit, you will probably have to call a family meeting to decide whether to adopt the cat or kitten, or, if there is a litter, how many, if any, to keep. This will no doubt be a vocal discussion, especially when there are kittens involved and you have small children (and sometimes not so small ones) in the house.

Once you have decided who stays and who goes, you have a number of choices for finding homes for your strays. If your find is obviously a house pet, you can put notices on area bulletin boards and run newspaper advertisements under "Pets Found." There is advertising on the Internet.

Showing the cats, rather than just talking about them or printing ads, can help enormously in finding them homes. Take the cat (or some littermates) in a carrier or two around to friends and neighbors—folks you know will provide good homes for them. One woman, looking to place a stray she could not keep, took it into her small office for a day, along with all the cat paraphernalia it needed. Sure enough, one of her coworkers adopted it. This works best, of course, in a small, rather informal office where you drive to work—and where you know your coworkers well enough to decide they can be trusted with the adoption.

In "interviewing" applicants from other sources, you will have to trust your judgment in deciding who will make a good caregiver for your stray. Other cats in the household could be a sign of commitment to pet care. Ask them where they plan to keep the cat—inside or outside? How many hours a day will the cat be alone? Watch these people as they become acquainted with the animal. Talk to them about spaying or neutering. They should agree to the surgery as soon as a vet says it can be done. It is better to do as the shelters do and not give your stray or kittens from a litter to people looking for Christmas presents, or any kind of gift, for others. Ask that the one whom the present is for come over in person to meet you and the cat.

"She Followed Me Home"

We have all seen television commercials and print ads with a cute child holding a cute dog or cat and saying just that, usually to Mom. Oh dear, what's a parent to do?

This can be a good learning experience for a child, and it might be an excellent opportunity for all of you to gain a new pet.

Some lessons your child can learn from you in this situation are:

➤ Just because you found it does not necessarily mean it is yours. The cat very likely has a home, with its owner feeling sad and missing it.

➤ It is your and your child's responsibility to try to find that owner.

➤ If no one responds, then keeping the cat might be a possibility. If, however, someone in your household is very allergic to cats or you feel you cannot afford the expense of a pet, you have to help the child understand that adoption is not possible.

If you do keep the cat, the youngster should know about the responsibility of a pet. Talk about how the cat needs to become familiar with your home and how it might be hiding a lot in the meantime. Cats sleep a good deal and should not be interrupted for play. Ask your child whether he or she will take on the chore of cleaning the litter box. (They will, of course, say "Yes, yes, absolutely," but sometimes that task eventually ends up with Mom.)

After talking over the practicalities of cat ownership, you can all settle back for an animated discussion about what to name the newcomer. That can take just seconds for some, but a l-o-n-g period of deliberation for others.

Don't Feel Guilty

If no one claims your stray, you cannot keep it yourself, and you have been unable to find a home for it, don't feel you have let the poor animal down. You can take it to a shelter, perhaps a facility where animals can stay for the rest of their lives. A veterinarian can give you the addresses of those places in your area.

What would be wrong is to turn the cat loose on the street or in the country, assuming it can fend for itself. It likely cannot, and this time, instead of being rescued by someone like you, it could suffer some misfortune or even be killed by a car or other animals.

It's Been Said

"The greatness of a nation can be judged by the way its animals are treated."

—Mahatma Gandhi

Chapter 3

Say "Ah"

In This Chapter

➤ A close-up look at the cat you are considering adopting

➤ Handicapped animals can thrive in a caring home

➤ That first trip to a veterinarian

➤ Whose cat? Make sure everyone knows it's yours

Whether you get your cat for $45 from a local humane society or pay $1,000 for a fancy one from an area breeder, it is important that you check the animal for obvious health problems before saying, "I'll take this one, please." You are less likely to encounter poor health with a breeder's cat than with one you are considering from a litter of strays, but it *can* happen.

Many problems with a new cat can be fixed, sometimes quickly, at a veterinary clinic. A smaller number are more serious. Some folks want a very ill cat in spite of the bad news they are handed; others return the cat. It is important to know your skills and limitations when considering adopting a pet that is not hale and hearty, so that you make the best decision for you and that animal.

What to Look For in a Healthy Cat or Kitten

There are some rudimentary checks you can make to ensure that the animal you want is healthy—or at least healthy enough to bring you to the next step in this adoption: seeing a veterinarian. Naturally, only a vet can tell you what's going on inside that little fuzzball.

Whether the cat is frisky and playing or is sitting off by itself will probably tell you more about the cat's temperament than whether it is sick or well, although, of course, a cat that is ailing will not be active.

A healthy cat has clear eyes. If its eyes are runny, it could be suffering from any number of ailments, ranging from an upper respiratory problem to feline distemper. Some of those illnesses are easily cleared up with medication; others are more daunting. Watch those eyes as you play with the animal. A cat whose eyes do not follow your moves could be visually impaired or even blind.

Sneezing is also a sign of illness, ranging again from a mild infection to a serious condition. The cat's nose should not be runny either. A cat's nose is normally cold and wet. One that is dry, unless the cat has been snoozing in the sun, could indicate that something is not quite right, perhaps a simple problem easily remedied with medication or proper nutrition.

Open the cat's mouth to check its teeth and gums. The teeth should be clean and white, the gums not red but a healthy pink. Also look for breathing that is quiet and even, not labored. While you are petting the cat, feel it through its fur. It ought to seem fleshy, not scrawny, but should not have a potbelly, which could be a sign of worms (something else that can be attended to by a vet).

You can clap your hands when the cat is looking away from you to see if it can hear properly, but cats being cats, yours might not turn because it just doesn't feel like it. A vet will have to examine it for possible hearing loss.

If you see specks of black when looking into the cat's ears, the animal probably has ear mites, which are quite common, especially in strays, and can be cleared up easily. A cat constantly scratching its ears or shaking its head is another indication of mites or perhaps of an ear infection.

The cat's coat should be shiny and clean. Part its fur to see if there is any sign of sores, hair loss, or other skin problems. If there seems to be something amiss, you do not need to be leery of taking that animal. Just jot down one more "must-see" for the vet.

While you are looking closely at the fur, check for little black spots the size of a pinhead. (Admittedly, this is a little hard to do with a black cat or one of another dark color!) The spots might appear on its face and around its rear quarters as well. These are flea feces. Yes, yuck. Actually, if the cat has fleas you might see one, or several, jump off its body. Fleas, which can quickly infest an entire house, can be seen to by a vet during your cat's first visit.

Fleas are only one of several good reasons for keeping your new cat separate from the other animals in your household until it has been carefully examined by a vet. We have suggested this strategy several times so far in this book, and it relates more to health concerns than possible hissy fits between your current pet and the newcomer.

If the cat you want seems fit and healthy after your inspection, you might want to take it with the proviso that if a serious problem arises from the vet's visit, you have the option of returning the animal.

Handicapped Cats Can Still Be Great

You will often see a handicapped cat put up for adoption. Perhaps it has lost a limb in a traffic accident, or its hind quarters are partially paralyzed. Maybe it is now blind, or it was born deaf, which the new owner did not realize. In any event, and for whatever reason, the owner of such a pet cannot keep the animal, and it winds up in a shelter cage.

You should know that a handicapped cat can enjoy life as much as a handicapped human can. We might shoot horses when a leg buckles, but cats and dogs do just fine running about with three legs and can even learn to navigate with partial paralysis. Blind and deaf cats need a bit of extra attention, but their quality of life in a good home is A-1. Pets with these handicaps, or chronic illnesses, can be high-spirited, curious, shy, affectionate, and every other adjective you can attach to a much-loved house pet.

Blindness might be a birth defect, but more often it results from illness or injury. If you decide to keep a cat you know is blind, it will, of course, have to remain indoors (unless you take it outside the house on a leash and watch it carefully). Gradually, with your help, the cat will learn furniture placement and the location of food and water bowls and the litter box. Remember, cats have an acute sense of both hearing and smell. Their whiskers will help guide them, too.

Talk often to your blind cat. Your voice will reassure it. Remember, in its dark world it will not know what—or who—is out there. Talk to it before you touch it too, so that you do not startle it. It *will* enjoy its life, thanks to the extra steps you and the others in your household take to consider its needs. More than one visitor has said to the owner of a few cats, "Which is the blind one?"

Deafness occurs occasionally in cats, and it is quite common in white cats with blue eyes. Many feel the deaf cat has less of a burden than the blind one, and, in fact, the cat that cannot hear maneuvers equally well in *its* world, which is a silent one. Your vet will help you acclimate your cat, suggesting, for example, that you might walk heavily coming up to it so that it can feel the vibrations of your approach. You can work out a system for letting the cat know its food is out, although many cats hang around the kitchen at mealtime and do not need you to announce "Soup's on."

Several cat (and dog) owners around the country have formed support groups for owners of handicapped pets and pets with serious illnesses. They exchange information on medical advances and household tips, and in general they are there for one another in a situation that is not common among pet owners. Ask your vet or local cat club if there is such a group near you. If the answer is no, why not start one? If you want nationwide membership, you can announce your intention in a letter to the editor of a cat magazine or on the Internet. For a local group, send a typed notice of your interest to veterinarians in a countywide or regional area for posting on their bulletin boards.

If you feel, after hearing the veterinarian's diagnosis about defects or other serious incapacitations, that you are unable to look after that cat the way it should be cared for, by all means return it. It could well be adopted by someone who can provide it with a loving home. Then, continue your search for the cat that's right for you.

Checking Out the Newcomer with a Vet

Most folks who have newly adopted a cat take it to a veterinarian within two or three days. One reason for the hurry is that the cat has been isolated from the rest of the household or not brought home at all, and the owner is eager to end that separation and get on with a normal life. Also, if there is a serious problem with the cat, the owner wants to know about it before forming too close an attachment to that animal. It might have to be returned to the shelter or other source.

Some shelters have a veterinary clinic on the premises, which makes it especially easy to have a cat examined. No doubt you already have a vet if you have other furry companions at home.

What the vet will do that you cannot is, of course, look at that animal with a more practiced eye and check the state of its health beyond what is obvious. The vet can also determine the approximate age of the cat if it is a stray. He or she can tell you if your new pet is male or female, if you do not know, and will also know if it has been spayed or neutered.

Your cat will receive its necessary vaccinations for rabies and distemper, and you will be on record with the vet for annual reminders.

A vet will also check the cat's heart rate, look into its eyes and ears, and take blood samples to check for any number of illnesses. Two of the most serious are feline immunodeficiency virus (FIV), which is a disease in cats that is similar to AIDS in humans, and feline leukemia virus (FeLV). Both are incurable (but keep in mind they are not transferable to humans).

What is important to know here is that many cats can lead a comfortable life for several years with FIV and FeLV, but should be kept indoors and separated from other felines in the house. For some owners that means a one-cat household, but other cats keep their FeLV or FIV cat on one floor and the other cats on another level, or they make some other arrangement that allows them to keep the ailing cat.

Sometimes you will be asked to leave your cat with the vet overnight for tests. Sometimes you will take it home, but must return the next day with a stool sample to be checked for worms and other internal parasites. As gross as worms sound—and they certainly *are* gross—that is yet another condition that need not deter you from adopting a particular animal. It can easily be treated.

How Many Toes Is Too Many?

Do you have cats living with you now? Quick, how many toes do they have? Have you ever checked? Many owners have not, and indeed do not know the normal number of digits. Is it five? Six? How many?

Five toes is usual; six, seven, and even eight are rare. Sometimes the extra toes are fully formed, while with other cats a bit of a toe might be almost buried behind another one.

Cat Language

A cat with extra toes has a condition known as **polydactylism**. It is the same name as a similar birth defect in humans.

Several years ago, the *Boston Globe* reported on a Boston University biologist who had conducted an interesting study. He determined that extra-toed cats could be traced to Boston's early settlement, where they arrived through immigration or on commercial sailing ships. Most ships did have cats aboard, either as pets or to deal with the rat population, and sailors might have deliberately chosen the extra-toed animals for their uniqueness. Docking in Boston and settling there, the cats bred, and eventually their offspring made their way through New England, Canada, and, to a lesser degree, other parts of the country.

On inspecting a sample of Boston cats, the professor found the multitoed syndrome in 12 percent of them. In New York City, however, which did not see a sizable migration from Boston, the professor found only two-tenths of 1 percent of the felines checked had more than five toes. Philadelphia also had a low number of those animals.

Interesting data, isn't it? One point to consider if you start counting the toes on your new feline and wonder when you will stop is that how many toes a cat sports has no bearing on its health.

That's My Cat!

Now that you have found and brought home this little treasure, you certainly do not want to lose it. But if somehow it does wander or become lost, you want to take any measure necessary to ensure its return to you.

It is wise to identify your cat, even though it lives indoors. Actually, many communities mandate some sort of identification in their cat licensing ordinance. You might have discovered that's the case where you live.

Pet ID can be particularly important in times of natural disasters, such as earthquakes, hurricanes, flooding, tornadoes, and hazardous substance leaks that sometimes force residents from their homes. Lost cats with identification are not mistaken for strays and stand a greater chance of being reunited with their owners. If you are leaving your animal with a friend when you evacuate the area, have that person's name and address on a separate ID tag along with your pet's permanent tag.

The simplest ID is a collar with a metal or heavy plastic tag. These cost around $5 and can be purchased at pet supply stores, at veterinary clinics, or through advertisements in cat magazines and cat supply catalogs.

Tabby Tips

Some estimates say only 2 to 4 percent of cats in a shelter are reunited with their owners. Proper ID could significantly increase that percentage.

You do not have to be afraid that your cat will choke on the collar. Simply purchase one marked "breakaway" or "with an escape feature" that will prevent this from happening.

If you do not want your name and address on the tag, you might have just your telephone number engraved. Some companies offer a registry service where you put *their* phone number on a tag and the call goes to that office. Their theory is if you lose your cat while traveling with it, there will be nobody to answer your home phone if someone calls. These companies advertise in cat magazines and in mail-order catalogs. Maybe you don't travel much and you do not want to spend the money for such a service, which costs about $20 to $30 a year. Then you can put your own phone number on the tag and skip the central service.

You might also tattoo your cat. You could use your address or pick an arrangement of numbers—perhaps your phone number. (Some folks use their Social Security number, but you may not want that in circulation.) A veterinary clinic or animal shelter can tattoo the number onto your cat. You can then register that number at all the shelters in your region. If you travel great distances with your cat, you might want to sign up with a company that offers a national registry, so your pet can be traced if it is lost anywhere in America.

A drawback here is that if your cat is turned in, shelters might not see, or have the time to look for, a tattoo. The marking could be buried under its fur. Also, if a local resident finds your cat, he or she might not know where to call about the tattoo (although if that individual does call a shelter where you are registered, you'll have your pet back).

One growing trend is the microchip. Here a veterinarian injects a pellet the size of a grain of rice under a cat's skin around its shoulder blades, a procedure no more painful than an inoculation. When the lost pet is found and, say, taken to a shelter, the shelter uses a scanner to pick up the chip and identify the animal.

The microchip is a solid means of identification, and surveys are beginning to show successful retrieval rates. However, there are still a few wrinkles to iron out. What if the cat is picked up by a resident of that community who believes it is a stray and does not know it has a microchip? Also, many, if not most, shelters and humane societies cannot afford a scanner for each microchip manufacturer. Companies are trying to cross-scan now, which means using scanners that can recognize chips from various manufacturers. That should alleviate incompatibility problems.

Microchipping costs $25 to $40 for a vet to implant, and registration at a manufacturer's computerized database costs another $15 to $35. Your vet can supply information about various microchip companies.

Imperfect as some means of ID are for a cat, any one of them is better than none and raises your chances of your pet's return if you become separated.

It's Been Said

"Even the smallest feline is a masterpiece."

—Leonardo da Vinci

Chapter 4

Welcome Home, Fur Face

In This Chapter

➤ Making room for the newcomer

➤ Helping your cat get along with other household pets

➤ Achoo! Is this wonderful cat making you sneeze?

So there's a new face around your place. What a difference that ball of fur will make in your life! No doubt you are already thinking how dull things must have been around the house before its arrival.

You will be busy for a while as you shop for your new pet, take it to the veterinarian, introduce it to everyone in your household (including your other animals), and generally help it make itself at home. Things will eventually settle down, although with a cat around, every once in a while you can expect the unexpected.

Cat Gear

If this is your first cat, you will incur a bit of an expense getting set up. When one woman told a friend that she was planning to get a cat, the friend exclaimed, "Oh, wonderful. I can give you a shower."

She was joking, but if this had been her pal's first time out with a pet she could have used the gifts. There is always something, practical or just fun, to give cat owners or the pets themselves.

For your newcomer, you will need water and food bowls, and they should be placed in a spot that is convenient for you and conducive to pleasant and leisurely eating for the cat. That means not in the path of traffic and not near the litter box.

Is there a dog in your household? You might find you have to feed your cat on a countertop or in some other area the dog cannot reach. Otherwise the dog will chomp away at the cat's food. One family put the cat bowls in their attached garage where there is a pet door leading from the kitchen. The door is too small for their Irish Setter to wriggle through.

Let's not forget buying the food itself. There is a discussion of what you might choose to feed your pet in Chapter 10.

You will also need some identification for your cat, a point raised in Chapter 3. What *don't* you need? If money is tight, forget about a cat bed. They are nice if you would like to spring for one, but you can fashion a bed out of blankets or odd pieces of fabric, sheets, or carpeting. Just make sure it is warm and cozy, and if possible give it some sort of cover or awning (such as a cardboard carton resting on its side). Cats love to feel they are hidden even when everyone can see them. Naturally, that bed should be kept in an area where the cat will not be disrupted by family members regularly passing through.

In any event, you are likely to find that where your cat really wants to snooze is on your bed. You will have to decide whether you will permit that. Pussy will also take its 14 or so naps a day on various chairs, sofas, and other comfy spots around your place, so buying a bed does not necessarily mean your cat will do all its dozing there.

You can also save a few dollars not buying toys. Yes, most cats love to play and need that physical and mental stimulation, but homemade toys, or those that are ready-made, such as paper bags, are easy enough to come by.

The Litter Box

Another purchase will have to be a litter box and some filler for it. Presumably your new cat already knows how to use the box. They learn that easily and quickly as kittens.

The box should be in a space in your home that allows the cat some privacy. Spread some newspapers under the box. If you want to protect the floor underneath, you can purchase a heavy, plastic, see-through floor mat at an office supply store, the kind placed under typists' chairs, and lay that down first with newspapers on top and the litter box on top of that. These mats cost around $12.

It is important to keep the litter box clean. Cats will often refuse to use a box that is dirty and opt instead to leave "deposits" around the house. Also, a dirty litter box smells.

The litter box should be cleared of solids daily, and some new litter should be added. Plastic scoopers are sold for that purpose, but they eventually snap in half. Instead, pick up a metal slotted ladle in the housewares section of the supermarket for $2 or $3. It will last forever and just needs washing when you have finished cleaning the litter box. The box ought to be washed with soap and water at least once a week, then filled with all-new litter to a depth of two inches.

By the way, unless the litter you buy is specifically marked biodegradable (and flushable), don't pour an entire box of used litter down a toilet or drain. It could cause blockage.

Tabby Tips

If you live alone, give some thought to how your pet would fare if something happened to you. You might want to give a neighbor a key to your home so he or she could feed your cat in an emergency. Carry a card with you that states you have a pet at home that needs care.

Those First Few Days

Cats have their own way of coping with the stress of entering a new household. When you put yours down on the floor for the first time, it might scurry under the sofa and stay there for hours, maybe days. Some cats will leap out an open window to get away. (Of course, you will have your windows closed or screened in anticipation of a fearful flight.)

It is hard to tell how your cat will be affected by its surroundings. Maybe this is its first home; perhaps this is its latest after several foster homes or a life on the street. The best way you can help your new pet become acclimated is by giving it plenty of quiet while it gets used to life at your place. That can be difficult, particularly for children, because everyone will want to look at the cat, talk to it, and play with it. Leave it alone, certainly if it is hiding. Even if it is walking around being inquisitive, try to let it wander at its own pace, although you will want to talk to it occasionally in a gentle tone. When it wants some attention, or as one owner put it, "when it needs to be purred," it will come to you. Cats catch a lot of Zzzzzs in a 24-hour day, and a stray, perhaps relaxing for the first time in its life, will spend a good deal of time sleeping now that it feels safe.

Introducing the Cat to Other Animals

"The fur will fly" is an expression that could be used when you are bringing home a new cat and you have one, two, or even more cats in your household.

Most of the time these situations work out well after two or three weeks. The cats sort themselves out into a new pecking order, and the newcomer takes its place in the fold. In the meantime, expect hissing, growling, fist fights, and cats chasing one another from room to room.

It is wise to keep the newcomer separate from the others for the first 48 hours or so. You can keep it in a bathroom or bedroom with its food, water, litter, and some toys. Because it will spend much time sleeping, it will not be lonesome. The other cats can smell the newcomer and hear it moving around through the door.

On the second or third day you might position the door so that it is open enough for everyone to meet and sniff, but not enough for a cat to slip in or out of that room. After a day, open the door and allow the newcomer freedom. Don't go out in those early days without putting the new cat back in its own quarters.

Other options include blocking off one floor for the "old" and one floor for the "new" cat, if you can do that where you live. You might also keep the newcomer in an animal cage for a few days with its food, water, and litter box so the other animals can see it and sniff around, but the cat is protected.

Some new cats are accepted easily in a multi-cat household with none of the dramatics. That is particularly true when the new member is a kitten. Sometimes, one cat tolerates the other but never really grows to like its housemate. Less frequently, an adjustment never comes. If, after four weeks or so, it looks as if there will never be tolerance in your household, let alone harmony, you have four choices: You can call in an animal behavior therapist to help everyone become adjusted; you can keep the cats separated forever, perhaps on different floors of your home; you can get used to the idea that one or more of the animals will never be happy about the newcomer (or the newcomer about the others) and learn to live with the occasional hissing or fighting; or you can return the new cat.

Cat Language

A group of cats is called a **clowder**, a group of kittens is called a **kendle**.

There are some felines that prefer to be in a one-cat household and never do adjust or even become at least reasonably accepting of another cat. It is not common, however, for an adoption to fail because of other cats in the house. Hang in there. It takes patience.

Now, about dogs. If you have a dog or two, again, you could have any one of several responses to and by the newcomer, depending on the temperament of each animal. Follow the preceding suggestions. Dogs and cats *can* get along well, although here too, it is usually a kitten that causes less fuss than an adult cat meeting your dogs.

Bringing Up Baby—and Your Cat

You are certainly a reasonable, rational person. But even sensible types, if they have a baby in the house or if one is on the way, could begin to wonder about old wives' tales about cats and babies. They suck the air from a baby's lungs, you have heard. They lap the milk from its lips.

Oh, those old wives; how they did babble. The truth is cats don't do that. What you might have to be concerned about is the cat that becomes stressed from a lack of attention at this busy time in new parents' lives. That pet could become listless and susceptible to illness. (If the baby is already present in the house when you bring in the cat, that is not likely to be the case, of course.) Pay extra attention to that animal now and after the baby arrives. Try smearing some baby lotion or oil that you will use with the infant on your hands now so the cat can become familiar with the scent. Let it smell the baby's blanket, too.

A spayed or neutered pet should be more docile than one with raging hormones. Still, it is wise not to leave your cat alone with your infant in the baby's first few weeks, but only because it could scratch the infant trying to get close to it to investigate—just investigate, not smother.

Tabby Tips

One very real danger while you are pregnant comes from *toxoplasmosis*, a disease that can be contracted by scooping and changing the litter box of an infected cat and that can affect a fetus's brain and nervous system. Try to have someone else in the household handle that chore. If that is not possible, use disposable gloves while cleaning the litter box and disinfect it frequently.

Could You Be Allergic?

Your eyes are misting as you pet your new cat, but it isn't emotion. Could you be allergic to that fur face?

You certainly could. Itchy eyes, a runny nose, and welts similar to mosquito bites on your arm where a cat accidentally scratched or bit you could all indicate an allergy.

The problem here is not cat hair, but the cat's saliva, which contains the allergen. When the cat grooms itself, the saliva is transferred to its fur, particles of which float in the air, settling on furniture, draperies, and the like and eventually reaching your lungs.

You do not have to get rid of your pet if you find you have an allergy to it. (An exception might be in a household where a child suffers from severe asthma.) Many allergists can tell you, rolling their eyes, about asthmatic cat owners they treat, some in multi-cat households.

What will not work is bathing your cat to keep the loose dander down. Also, too-frequent vacuuming just stirs up the particles of cat allergen, causing you more distress.

You can try over-the-counter antihistamines and decongestants. If that does not help, or if your symptoms become worse, it is best to visit an allergist. There could be other irritants in your life besides your cat, such as greenery or certain foods. The allergist can suggest shots, or if your condition turns out to be asthma, prescribe medications to try to keep it in check. The doctor will also have suggestions for making your home as allergen-free as possible.

It's Been Said

"A house without a cat, and a well-fed, well-petted, and properly revered cat, may be a proper house, perhaps, but how can it prove its title?"

—Mark Twain

Chapter 5

Cats Up Close

In This Chapter

➤ Physical traits that make a difference

➤ The secrets of working feet

➤ How cats groom themselves

➤ The five senses—feline version

➤ Purr facts

You don't have to do a Gallup poll to know that we humans admire cats. Even those people who protest (both loudly and often) that they hate cats often make pro-cat choices. In fact, cat admiration might just be one of the most dependable driving forces in our economy. Will it be a Lynx, a Cougar, or a Jaguar for you?

What is it that we admire? The graceful body line of the cat sitting proudly on a window sill? The silent stealth and focused control of the hunting cat? The almost analytical ability to leap and land exactly on target? The drive that keeps them clean? The love they purr?

Let's take a little time to become familiar with the masterpiece that is the cat.

The Body Beautiful

Grace, flow, and warm soft fur. What else could anybody want?

Well, being human, you might want to know *why* cats are so graceful and agile. Dogs and cats have virtually identical arrangements of their vertebrae (the bones in their spines). So why can a cat leap more than five times its own height? Or jump straight backward when startled? Or twist its body smoothly around seemingly impossible obstacles? Or right itself when falling and land on its feet? A dog can't.

Like some of the more agile breeds of dogs, the bones of the cat are both strong and light, and the body is very well muscles. What makes the cat really different, however, is a flexible skeleton. Feline vertebrae are connected by muscles rather than ligaments. These powerful muscles allow the cat's backbone to flex, extend, and even twist.

Tabby Tips

Cats beat out humans if you're counting bones in the skeleton. The human body contains 206 bones, while the cat body contains 230!

Although pet cats in ancient Egypt may have been some-what larger, domestic cats haven't really changed much during the 8,000 years that they've lived with humans. Today, most of them weigh about 10 pounds, with a few heavyweights topping 20 pounds. They all have short faces and small broad skulls. Their coats vary from virtu-ally hairless, to short hair (the most common), to long hair. Their coat colors range from white to black with lots of variations of orange and brown in between.

Unlike the scene in the dog kingdom where human con-trol over breeding has produced both the Toy Poodle and the Great Dane, human attempts to breed for midgets and giants in the cat kingdom have been pretty much unsuc-cessful. The silhouette of a cat in the window is the same the world over.

On Balance

There she is! Desdemona's walking the top board of the neighbors' fence again. She moves just as though it were a two-foot-wide sidewalk!

How does she do it? Some would say the cat's tail acts much like the balancing pole carried by a human tight-rope walker. This is true, but that's only a small factor in the ease and careless grace of a cat walking a fine line.

More important is the cat's highly developed sense of bal-ance, which is located in the inner ear. Like most crea-tures, the cat bases its movements on what it sees, but it also *subconsciously* corrects and augments vision with lightning-fast balance messages from the inner ear to the brain. It's this balance mechanism that helps the cat who falls or is dropped to land on its feet, usually unharmed.

The routine for righting is instinctual and the same for every cat. When dropped upside down, the cat brings its front legs close to its head while spreading its hind legs. Then, using both vision and inner ear balance, the cat bends at the waist and turns the front part of its body a full half circle to bring the head and front feet into a ground-facing position. The spine and hind legs twist to follow and the cat arches its back and extends its legs, ready to meet the ground. All this takes less than half a second!

Tabby Tips

The cat's righting procedure seems to work only when a cat falls from a horizontal position. A cat *can* be injured by a fall. Some studies show that cats have somewhat better odds when falling farther because they have more time to right themselves and their spread legs catch more air and act a bit like a parachute. However, there's no accurate way to predict whether a cat will be hurt from a fall.

But excellent balance and an amazing righting instinct still don't completely explain the careless grace of a cat walking the thin edge of a board. A few humans and some dogs can do it, but they have to *think* about putting one foot directly in front of another. Cats don't.

When walking naturally, the front paw prints of a cat line up right, left, right, left, one *directly behind* the other on an imaginary line that would be under the midline of the cat's body. The hind legs don't come in quite so close, but two inches is enough width for careless comfort.

Paws for Thought

The cat's feet are a thing of beauty, power, and awe. And they are precision-designed for a utilitarian function. No cat has ever said, "Oh, my aching feet!"

Cats walk on their toes. In fact, the soles of their feet rarely touch the ground. Now, this would obviously be uncomfortable for bears and humans, but design is everything, and it works just fine for cats. Their feet are shorter and narrower than the feet of other animals their size who walk on the soles of their feet. Their foot bones are also thinner and lighter, and those hard-working toes are very well padded.

The feet of the cat are a dead giveaway to its hunting heritage. Cats can walk silently because their paw pads are soft and pliant. Their retracted claws never click on a hard surface like a dog's nails. Fur between the pads and on the foot muffles sound even further.

All members of the cat family, except the cheetah, have retractable claws (which is why the touch of a cat foot can be soft and gentle or formidable indeed). The claws are worked by tendons and ligaments in the cat's foot. When the cat is relaxed, the tendons are relaxed and the claws are hidden under the skin and held in place by a ligament. When the cat tightens certain muscles, the tendons and the ligaments in the foot stretch and the claws come forward.

All cats sharpen their claws and scratch. But honestly, they don't do it to redesign your furniture or to thin the pile on your carpet. It's instinct. In the wild, claws are hunting tools and must remain sharp. Claws are also tools for territorial marking. In Africa, the scratched tree trunk is a "No Trespassing" sign to another lion. So don't be too hard on Mephistopheles when he experiments beyond the scratching post.

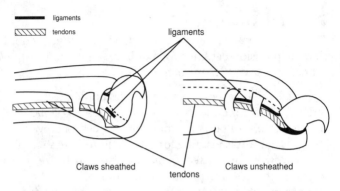

Weapons drawn at will: Tough tendons and ligaments stretch upon command from the brain to extend the cat's claws. It takes microseconds!

Cats also use their front paws for grooming their faces. This is a very important cat activity, and some cats become quite artistic (and compulsive) in its execution.

At the other end of the spectrum, paw pads are another tool (besides scratching and urinating) to mark one's territory. The marking is done through scent glands located on the cat's paw pads. You've probably seen a cat or two standing on its hind legs and pressing its front feet against a doorjamb or your leg. The cat is imprinting its scent.

And finally, cat paw pads sometimes serve a purpose similar to that of human sweat glands. The rich capillary blood supply in the pads helps to regulate body temperature. When a cat's body temperature rises, the capillaries dilate and dissipate heat. Sometimes you'll even see moist cat footprints on a cool surface.

Tabby Tips

Cats are sensitive to certain chemicals found in fertilizers, insecticides, paints, automotive products, and even the salts thrown on sidewalks in winter. In addition to ingesting these poisons when licking themselves for grooming, toxic amounts can be absorbed through their paw pads.

That Sandpaper Tongue

Most cat lovers agree that "sandpaper" is an apt description for the touch of even the most gentle pussycat's tongue. Being licked by a cat is not a pleasant sensation.

Like its feet, the cat's tongue is multifunctional and very efficiently designed for the survival of the species. It gets that sandpaper quality from the tiny barbs (almost like hooks) that cover its surface. These *papillae* help predatory cats clean every bit of flesh from the bones of their prey.

Are these tiny barbs useless or a nuisance to our pet cats? Hardly! The backward-pointing hooks are an important asset to the grooming process because they catch and pull dead hair, dirt, and parasites from the coat. They're also a stimulator to new life. The sandpaper quality of the mother cat's tongue probably irritates her newborn kittens. Their protesting cries often clear their lungs and start normal breathing. The licking of kittens' anal areas also helps to start urination and defecation.

The cat's tongue is also its portable goblet. Thin and pliant at the edges, it curls inward to make a fine drinking vessel. After each four or five laps, the cat will swallow.

As a tasting tool, the cat's tongue seems to be both specialized and idiosyncratic. It can detect even slight changes in the taste of water but has little or no ability to detect sweetness. And, as every cat owner knows, somewhere in the taste buds of the individual tongue are preferences for which there is no accounting. Cat tastes have been known to include cantaloupes and cockroaches, whipped cream and oysters. Of course, there's always room for a good mouse.

Cleanliness Is Next to Catliness

A child, a dog, and a cat come into the house on a rainy March afternoon. The child stands there dripping. The dog shakes, splattering the rain and mud about. The cat disappears, only to be seen again (after the muddy mess by the door is cleared away) sitting atop the coffee table as pristine as a porcelain statue.

Cats are known for their cleanliness. All members of the cat family (even the big hunting cats) groom themselves every day, and all wash their faces with their paws.

The tongue is the cat's grooming tool. Because of its flexible spine, the cat can reach most body parts with its tongue without undue effort. But not the face and ears. To clean their faces, cats apply saliva to a paw and then use that paw like a wet washcloth, rubbing in ever larger circles until they are satisfied with their cleanliness.

Cats need only be shown the location of the litter box and they'll use it, cleaning themselves afterwards. In fact, cats are so fastidious that they even meticulously clean their genitals after sex. (Perhaps that, too, should be added to the long list of traits responsible for the survival of the species!)

Electronic Ears, Almost

Ear wiggling in humans is usually a comedy routine, for those of us who can, that is. Ear turning in cats is a finely honed survival skill.

Most humans have six muscles associated with the outer ear, and the ears are stationary. Cats have between 20 and 30 muscles, depending on the type of cat, and each ear can rotate independently of the other up to 180 degrees (a half circle). Cats use their outer ears as cone-shaped receptacles to gather sounds to be processed by their brains.

And they gather a lot more sounds than we do. Both humans and cats hear in the lower range down to about 20 cycles per second. In the high range, however, human hearing stops at about 20,000 cycles per second (near the highest notes of a violin). Cat hearing can continue up to 60,000 cycles! That's why *they* hear the squeak of a mouse while *we* sit totally unaware. Mice, by the way, can hear sounds up to 95,000 cycles per second.

Tabby Tips

No bells, please! A tinkling bell on a cat's neck may warn unwary birds, but it also interferes with the cat's hearing. The sounds can be disorienting, and they are as annoying to the cat as wearing a mask with tiny eye slits might be to a human.

Besides having a wider sound range than humans, cats can hear better. The human auditory nerve has about 30,000 fibers; the cat's nerve has about 40,000. So don't be surprised if Felix gets unsettled whenever teenaged

Kevin or Debbie plays their favorite rock music on the boom box. Either separate quarters or a lower volume is probably a good idea.

Catching the Scent

Cats in the wild do not track prey by scent. And domestic cats are more responsive to the sound of a can opener than the smell of fish cooking for dinner.

Does that mean that cats do not have a well-developed sense of smell? Not at all. They just choose to use what works best for them when hunting: sight and sound. They seem to reserve their sense of smell for recognition and for pure pleasure.

What message the brain registers as a *smell* depends upon olfactory cells. Humans, who can't scent-recognize anything much beyond bread baking in the oven, have about 5 to 20 million olfactory cells. Dogs, who can track by scent alone, have 100 to 300 million. Cats fall in between, with 60 to 80 million.

Besides catnip, many cats have certain smells that they "just love." There's a whole society of patrician cats that have distinct preferences among upscale perfumes. Then there's the blue-collar group, who will try to crawl into a shoe just as soon as it's empty of a human foot.

There are people who say that some cats will knock over vases because they love the odor of the stagnant water inside. At the other extreme, you'll see cats hanging around swimming pools, probably enjoying the chlorine odor. Does it make sense? No, but your cat will let you know what it likes.

While the sense of smell seems to serve a hedonistic function in day-to-day cat life, it also serves as a means of recognizing and differentiating what is familiar and what is strange. And it definitely plays an important role in the *ongoing* survival of the species. Yes, sex. A healthy tom can catch the natural perfume of a ladyfriend who might just be receptive to him over a distance that is greater than the length of a football field.

Cats also have an auxiliary scent organ called the Jacobson's organ, located on the roof of their mouths. When they use it, they make a kind of funny grimace with their mouths, called *flehmen*. What they're doing is passing scent molecules over the organ to actually taste the scent.

Cat's Eyes

Large for the size of their heads, lustrous, and expressive, cat eyes mesmerize their adoring humans. We see in them a huge range of emotions and motivations, including love, anger, joy, curiosity, pain, embarrassment, hunger, and the urge to kill.

Beautiful as they are, cat eyes are designed for the hunt. They can detect minuscule movements in the distance, and they can quickly adjust to changes in the amount of available light. Their vertical pupils can narrow to thin slits in bright light and widen to as much as half an inch in very low light. Their eyelids can move up and down to close either partially or completely over the eye, and they secrete a lubricating fluid to smooth this movement along.

Cats also have a so-called "third eyelid," actually named the *nictitating membrane,* on each eye. It protects the eye and perhaps controls light with thin, pliable tissue that unfolds from the inner corner of the eye. In the healthy cat, this membrane usually cannot be seen.

Besides their extraordinary light sensitivity and movement perception, it was finally proven in the 1960s that cats *can* see color. However, they don't seem to care much whether a mouse is gray or brown.

Contrary to popular belief, cats *cannot* see in total darkness. It just seems that way. On a night that we humans would consider total darkness, cat pupils dilate very wide to enable them to use every bit of available light. When sudden light, whether from a fiery torch or car headlights, strikes these wide open pupils, the cat's eyes glow in the dark. This has gotten cats into trouble over the ages because the eerie effect has been associated with evil, magic, and the supernatural. In fact, the glow is the reflection of light on the retina at the back of the cat's eye.

What Whiskers Do

How do cats get around in very dark places? They use their whiskers!

The cat has four rows of whiskers on each side of its face. The upper two rows can move independently of the lower rows, but all whiskers are sensitive to even minute changes in air currents. You might say that the cat "feels" its way with its whiskers.

Because they usually extend beyond the width of their bodies, cats also quite literally use their whiskers as feelers. With these magic sensing rods, they can test their ability to fit through small places and get around obstacles.

Purr-fect

Well, cats do seem to be quite the perfect hunters. But there's this one extra feature. Why do cats purr?

No one really knows. But we do know *when* cats purr, and we think we know *how*. We also know cats are the *only* animals that purr.

Most people believe that purring is a sign of contentment and even affection. It probably is. Who hasn't enjoyed the purr of the warm cat curled in your lap? Or looked up from the newspaper because the cat is purring so loudly by the fire?

Cats also purr in situations that are not exactly warm and fuzzy. Newborn kittens purr as they suck for their mother's milk, which may be pleasant for them because they're getting nourishment, but it's also hard work for so young an organism. Grown cats often purr loudly when they are anxious, in distress, or in pain. Sometimes, a veterinarian attempting to examine a cat can't hear the heartbeat because the cat is purring so loudly. Some female cats in labor purr. And there are many reports of cats who purred while dying.

For ages many people believed that purring was something like snoring, done while breathing, or something like growling, done with the vocal chords. But it's not. Cats purr with their mouths closed. Most experts believe that the sound is created by two folds of membrane behind the vocal chords, sometimes called the false vocal chords. Like all other cat vocalizing, purring can change in intensity and in pitch. We still don't completely understand it.

It's Been Said

"Like a graceful vase, a cat, even when motionless, seems to flow."

—George F. Will

CatSpeak

Many people go to college to study communication arts, which is really all about how to get messages from one living being to another. Yet without a college diploma (saving loving caregivers many thousands of dollars), cats manage to communicate very well indeed. They even leap effortlessly across language barriers. In fact, a cat can usually teach a human to understand everything that needs to be understood in a matter of days.

Cats also communicate with other cats with tremendous facility. A Maine Coon can tell an Egyptian Mau exactly what she thinks of him, and a Cornish Rex and an Alley

Cat can be best friends. Even dogs and other animals quickly pick up enough cat language to get the major messages.

How do they do it? Let's take a short course in cat communication.

Let Me Tell You How I Love You

There are people who say that cats are not affectionate animals. Most of them have never really known a cat. Without ever fawning or begging, without expressing false feelings in expectation of a reward, cats show their thoughts and emotions in genuine, even if usually subtle, behaviors.

The purr is to the cat what the smile is to humans: a characteristic of the species, a sign of contentment, and a means of social communication. The cat purring to your touch is expressing both pleasure and friendliness.

Unlike humans, however, cats also mark what they feel is their own (what they would keep and protect) with their scent. Scent glands are located on the face, behind the ears, in the tail area, and in the feet, and cats use them all. A cat rubbing its body around and against your legs is expressing affection by expressing possession. It wants to keep you. The same goes for a cat who stretches its full length to plant two front feet as high on your leg as possible.

Even more a sign of affection is a cat rubbing its face against your skin. The cat is marking you lightly with scent, but, more importantly, it is telling you that pleasing you is important. The cat who rubs its face against another cat is expressing both submission and the desire to please.

And then there is gift giving. Just as humans give roses for Valentine's Day and monogrammed golf balls for a birthday, cats give presents to express their affection. Greatly valued in the eyes of the cat are dead frogs on your pillow at dawn or field mice on your doorstep. Don't forget to say "Thank you!"

The Eyes Have It

Some people believe the eyes are a mirror of the mind and read from them both thoughts and feelings. When it comes to cats, there is no way of knowing the accuracy of human readings, except perhaps with your own individual cat. We do have a good deal of information, however, on how a cat's eyes appear in certain situations.

When a cat is interested, attentive, calm, and friendly, its eyes are opened wide but not strained to the maximum width, and its pupils are in normal response to the available light. When a cat is frightened, the eyes strain wider and the pupils dilate. When a cat is feeling aggressive or wants to frighten or intimidate, its eyes will narrow into a focused stare. When it is hunting or stalking, its eyes are wide open but very focused and unmoving.

The use of the focused, unblinking stare in both cat hunting and pre-aggression probably accounts for the fact that cats do not like to be stared at by humans. Many cats will respond with quick blinking and turning the head to one side (away from the staring person).

Tabby Tips

If you are meeting a fearful or timid cat, try catching its gaze, fixing your attention, closing your eyes in a very slow blink, and opening them again, also very slowly. Some experts believe this action eases tension, intimidation, and anxiety in the cat.

But long, slow, controlled blinking—that's another story in the cat world. In her book *The New Natural Cat,* Anita Frazier makes a case for the slow blink as a sign of contentment and affection, a kind of "cat kiss." She claims it works as a communication device both between cats and humans and cats and other cats.

Ear Signals

Whereas human ears are not much more than turned-out flaps, cat ears are almost weather vanes to the prevailing winds of the cat's thoughts. They can move independently of each other, turn a half circle, perk up, hit the horizontal, and go flat. Each position has meaning.

A cat hearing sounds totally inaudible to its human companion might turn one ear toward the source to hear better. Or perhaps hearing a sound in front of it, the cat might turn both its ears slightly forward just as it focuses its eyes.

Cats' amazing hearing and control of their ears, however, may contribute to the bad cat reputation of being inattentive. When you talk to your dog, he'll usually lift his head. Your cat may respond to your voice simply by adjusting the angle of her ears.

A contented, trusting, calm cat will carry its ears up, forward, and slightly to the side. A fearful cat will hold its ears in a horizontal position, out from the sides of its head. An aggressive or defensive cat will pin its ears back against its head. The hunting cat carries its ears up and pointed forward.

Whisker Signs

Cat whiskers are much more than bristle-like face hair. They are guiding tools sensitive to touch, vibrations, and some say even sound waves. And since the top rows are moveable, it follows that they respond to the situations in a cat's life.

A cat walking with its whiskers pointed only slightly forward and down might be attentive, but it is also calm. When the whiskers are pointed forward and up, it is a sign that the cat is excited or anxious. Even more forward, up, and bristled indicates a defensive or aggressive situation.

About Your Hair, Kitty

Besides humans, no animal is so concerned about the condition and appearance of its hair as the cat. Cats have an excuse, however, because the coat does more than contribute to cat beauty. It also provides warmth in winter and insulation in summer. *And* it is a defense mechanism.

When a cat is afraid, it makes itself look bigger by puffing out its coat, especially its tail. Each hair stands out as if electrified. Much like the porcupine's hooked quills, this body language is saying, "Don't mess with me!" But the cat's expansion is all just show.

The aggressive or defensive cat who is meeting a challenger might not want to show fear by fluffing itself up. Instead, it will raise the fur over its shoulders, called the hackles, to let the adversary know he should take the challenge seriously.

Tail Talk

The cat's highly developed nervous system extends to the tip of its tail. Sensitive and responsive, that tail is often a signal mechanism for a cat's mood and motivation. Watch it and it will give you messages.

Take "Welcome home!" for example. Your dog will jump up and down, barking gleefully, running in circles around you. Your cat will come out of hiding at a trot, head up, eyes bright, tail erect. In fact, carrying the tail high over the body is always a sign of cat contentment and maybe even a bit of self-satisfaction.

The welcoming cat.

Another common message might be "What's going on here?" or "I'm not sure I like all this." The threatened or nervous cat will hold its tail low and whip it back and forth.

When hunting or stalking, the cat will also hold its tail low, but absolutely motionless except for a possible tiny twitch at the last vertebrae. It's almost as if all the force of control for the tensed muscles must escape somehow through the tip of the tail.

Only when a cat is defeated and fearful will it carry its tail down between its legs. Even the frightened cat who is still ready to fight lifts the tail and puffs it out.

Often, the cat protects its sensitive tail by wrapping it around its feet when sitting or around its body when lying down. At other times, however, when the cat is sleeping or completely relaxed, it will allow the tail to hang down over the edge of a shelf or a countertop or just extend out from its body on the floor. At these times, there's always the danger the tail will be stepped on or shut in a door.

Body Language

There have been many pop psychology and self-help books written on human body language. That's because how we do something often means something other than what we're doing. It's not nearly so complicated with cats. They just do what they do consistently in response to the situation.

Let's take arching the back, for example. This cat act has more than one meaning, but the situation and the manner in which the arching is done will always tell you what the arching means. It's sort of like the words *no* and *know* or *not* and *knot;* they can't be differentiated by their sound, but we don't get them mixed up because of usage.

When a cat arches its back softly and slowly, it is usually to greet you with affection, especially if it is also rubbing against your legs. If it arches its back while you are petting it, the cat is probably luxuriating in the pleasure of the moment. If it arches its back after a nap, it is probably just stretching. But when it arches its back while standing on stiff legs with its hair bristling, it is either frightened or about to fight.

Then there's tapping with a paw. Imagine Griselda sitting on your desk and batting at the pen while you write. She just wants to play. If she extends the claws and adds a little more power, the gentle pat becomes a swipe. Swipes give warning or reaffirm the cat social order in the home and in the wild.

Outdoors, the crouch with its tense, motionless muscles is indicative that the cat is about to attack its prey. In the home, that same crouch with all its gathered energy usually means that your cat is about to pounce on a toy.

The best body language, the position that most delights cat owners and observers alike, is the cat's ultimate relaxation pose. There he is, Thunder Toes, on his back, legs outstretched, belly exposed, not a care or concern in the world. This is total trust, total comfort. In the wild, however, a cat exposing its soft underside to an enemy is making a sign of submission, or an admission of defeat.

It's a great life after all! (Holly Carter)

Meow Meow

Because cats make sounds that have specific meanings, many experts say that the sounds constitute a kind of language. Studies of cat vocalization show that there are up to 100 different sounds in the cat's vocabulary. In fact, academic studies have been conducted to classify the sounds by vowels and consonants and to record their meanings. But anyone who's lived with a cat has no need of a study. You know when your cat is asking for food, wants to go out, is anxious, or is in pain.

Sometimes you'll see your cat making mouth motions as if it were meowing, but there is no sound. Well, you've been fooled. There is a sound, it's just out of the range of human hearing. We call it the *silent meow*. Other cats can hear it just fine.

Yes, cats talk. They also understand. Experts estimate that with training and repetition, cats can be taught to respond to 25 to 50 words. They might not always respond exactly as we want them to, but they do respond.

No Words Needed

Humans make sounds that communicate without words: screams, grunts, sighs, moans, and so on. Cats do too, and their variety, range, and volume for so small an animal is truly magnificent. For cats, these communication devices work well from cat to human and even better from cat to cat.

Growls, from low to rumbling, are threats or signs of anger. Hisses and spits communicate displeasure and dislike far beyond a reasonable doubt. On the other hand, sounds called chirping and cooing, for want of better words, indicate pleasure or some specific message. They're often used by mother cats with their kittens.

Sometimes when cats watch prey through a window, you'll hear a kind of chattering of the jaws. This is not considered an aggressive sound, but rather something like anticipation. Toms approaching girlfriends also do it.

Cats under stress, traveling in a cat crate, for example, will make a continuous series of long moans quite different from their normal range of communication devices. The sound obviously does not indicate pain, but rather intense displeasure and also frustration at the inability to escape.

Caterwauling

The dictionary definition of *caterwaul*, to make a harsh cry or to quarrel noisily, applies to humans, but who doesn't think of cats calling in the night whenever the word is used!

The common misconception is that the cats are howling in love calls. Nothing could be further from the truth. The raucous noise that is commonly called caterwauling is made by tom cats discussing territorial rights.

When female cats scream, it is an entirely different sound and is usually associated with sex.

Talking with Your Cat

Some cats, such as the Siamese, tell you more than you ever wanted to know. Their conversation seems constant during their waking hours and sometimes during your sleeping hours. Many cats, however, rarely say more than "I'm hungry."

And from the cat's perspective, so it is with humans, too. Some talk a lot and some hardly ever. "Why bother? They can't understand us," say some talk-not-to-the-cat people.

Most experts agree that it is a good idea to talk to your cat. Cats understand more than you might think. They read our body language just as we read theirs. And cats can often sense human emotions. Most important, however, talking with your cat reinforces the bond between you and your feline friend.

It's Been Said

"A cat has absolute emotional honesty; human beings, for one reason or another, may hide their feelings, but a cat does not."

—Ernest Hemingway

Chapter 7

It's Hereditary!

In This Chapter

➤ The importance of genes

➤ Coat color and texture

➤ Classifying the body beautiful

➤ Introducing some breeds

Eric Gurney, an American cartoonist, once said, "The really great thing about cats is their endless variety. One can pick a cat to fit almost any kind of decor, color scheme, income, personality, mood. But under the fur, whatever color it may be, there still lies, essentially unchanged, one of the world's free souls."

What makes the Norwegian Forest Cat different from the Egyptian Mau, the British Shorthair different from the Burmese, and the Himalayan different from the Siamese?

The answer is in the genes.

What's a Gene?

In the 19th century (the 1870s and 1880s to be specific), the abbot of an Augustinian cloister in Austria began to study the source of the different shades of green among the edible peas that grew in the monastery garden. He was Gregor Johann Mendel (1822–1884), and his work with hybrid plants formed the basis for the modern science of genetics.

Genetics is the study of heredity—how traits and characteristics (eye color, hair texture, and body type, for example) are passed from parents to offspring. Genes are the substances that determine these traits. Humans, cats, and all other animals get them on the chromosomes, half from the mother and half from the father, that unite in the first cell of conception.

A gene can be dominant or recessive. Let's take length of coat in cats as an example. The gene for long hair is recessive; the gene for short hair is dominant. So a kitten conceived with a longhaired and a shorthaired gene will have short hair. She will carry the recessive gene, however, and some of her offspring may be longhaired cats if she mates with a tom who has long hair or who is also carrying the recessive gene. In other words, it takes either one dominant gene or two recessive genes to produce the trait.

Why is all this important in cats? Because genes determine markings, color, coat, body type, breed, and personality. If you are looking for a kitten, you can learn a lot about what the future holds from its parents. If you plan to breed your cat, you can make choices that will affect the litter.

A Tiger Trait

One of the most common coat colorations seen in both pedigreed and non-pedigreed cats is the striped and spotted pattern we call *tabby*. These markings have been inherited through thousands of years from the cat's wild ancestors. Only recently, however, has genetic research pinned down the source of the pattern and color changes to a gene commonly called the *agouti* gene.

We see cats with the agouti gene as striped or spotted because each of their hairs is banded with alternating light and dark colors. The form of the banding and the amount of pigment (somewhere on the sliding scale between black and yellow) determine the pattern we see—in other words, whether your pet looks like a tiger or a leopard.

Shades and Smokes

Many cats look as though they are a solid color until some movement allows our eyes to catch waves of white coat close to the skin. The individual hairs in the coats of such cats are not banded in patterns like the tabby, but change color only once at some point along the shaft.

When only the outer 25 percent or so of each hair is colored (leaving most of the hair shaft close to the skin white), it's called a shade. When 50 to 80 percent of the shaft is colored (leaving from 20 to 50 percent close to the skin white), it's called a smoke.

Shade and smoke coats come in most colors, even black. They do not, however, come in red or cream, which always have an underlying tabby pattern to some degree. And of course, they can't be all white.

The One-Color Cat

The solid color cat is the result of a mutation (which is a spontaneous change in the genotype) of the agouti (tabby) gene, followed by human control over breeding. Cats of one color do not have the agouti gene of their wild ancestors.

Some solid color cats, the Siamese for example, are pointed. A pointed cat has a light-colored body and darker hair on the points. The word *points* refers to the nose, ears, tail, lower legs, and paws.

Cats that are solid white carry a dominant color-blocking gene that keeps pigment out of the skin and hair. This gene also causes blue, green, copper, or sometimes odd-colored eyes (each eye is a different color). It commonly results in deafness in one or both ears in blue-eyed and occasionally copper-eyed cats.

White with Other Colors

Different from the dominant white gene, another gene, commonly called the white-spotting gene, is present when cats have colored coats that are also marked with various degrees of white. The colored areas may be tabby patterned, shades, smokes, or solids. The white areas are pigment-free.

You've surely known at least one cat named Mittens or Boots. He or she was probably an example of this gene at work with minimal white (less than 25 percent of the body) appearing. Naturally, scientists called this the *mitted* manifestation.

Cat Language

A cat somewhere between one-third and two-thirds white is called a **bi-color**. A cat more than two-thirds white with some colored patches is called a **harlequin** or a **van**.

Tortoiseshell and Calico

Which is which? The two names are commonly mixed up.
The generally accepted differentiation is that the tortoiseshell is a black cat with red and/or orange markings
and some white, while the calico is a white cat with
patches of red, orange, and black. More important, however, the tortie has a mottled coat coloring, not distinct
patches like a calico.

Most tortoiseshell and calico cats are female. When the
rare male is found, he is usually sterile.

What About the Hair?

Because the gene for short hair is dominant in cats, it's
not at all surprising that there are more shorthaired cats
than any other kind. Most mixed-breed cats (cats the British affectionately call "moggies") are shorthaired.

Among pedigreed cats, however, coat is a prime consider-
ation and short hair has a lot of competition. Much careful breeding has gone into creating and maintaining
breed-specific coat qualities. Besides length, texture and
thickness are also characteristics that enter into show
judging.

Most longhaired cats are descendants or varieties of the
Persian, whose thick winter hairs can be as long as five
inches. At the opposite end of the spectrum, the Sphynx
has a coat so fine and short that it's usually called "hairless." Two British breeds, the Cornish Rex and the Devon
Rex, have coats curly enough to have come right out of
the beauty parlor. Examples of rougher coats can be seen
in the American Wirehair, the Norwegian Forest Cat, the
Maine Coon, and the Chartreux.

Body Types

Lots of us still don't want to accept the idea, but it's a fact:
Not only height but also weight and bone density are

pretty much determined by genes in both cats and humans (and other animals, too). In other words, you and your cat are probably going to have a body type a lot like your respective parents. Because of recessive genes, however, there's always the outside possibility that either of you might also take after a distant relative.

Predictions regarding probable body weight, size, and shape are usually more accurate for purebred cats than predictions about the human body or the mixed-breed cat body because there are far fewer unknown recessive genes in the pool. Most cat fanciers discuss their cats' body types within the following groups:

➤ *Cobby:* Short, sturdy cats like the Persian. They have a compact body, a deep chest, and a broad head. Humans like them might be called "stocky."

➤ *Semi-cobby:* Somewhat longer, but not quite so sturdy as the cobby cat. The American Shorthair is an example. Humans like them might be called "average" or "medium" build.

➤ *Muscular:* Quite long, but with good sturdy bones. The Egyptian Mau and the Havana are good examples. In human terms, we'd probably say "athletic."

➤ *Foreign:* Long, elegant cats like the Abyssinian. Their bodies are slender; their tails are long. We might say a woman like them is "lithe" or "svelte"; a man could be called "wiry."

➤ *Oriental:* Very long and elegant like the Siamese. "Intriguing" and "sinuous" might be good descriptive words for humans of this type.

➤ *Substantial:* Large, sturdy cats like the Maine Coon or the Ragdoll. About humans, we'd just say "big and tall."

Personality Counts!

Many people have tried to associate personality traits in cats to their coat colors. You may have heard that black cats are lovers (or roamers) and that white cats are sensitive. Some say that orange cats are comedians and black-and-whites just want to play all the time.

In fact, no study has proven any of these associations. The personality of the pet cat will probably be somewhat like that of one or both of its parents, but there's no guarantee. The odds are better among the purebreds where there are at least known tendencies within the breed.

Cat Breeds

Cat registries and cat fanciers' groups are growing throughout the world. Many countries have several different organizations, which in turn recognize and register different breeds. Today, there are more than 50 cat breeds in the United States alone. And believe it or not, that number is still growing, both here and abroad, as knowledge of genetics allows breeders to emphasize selected traits.

Introducing you to every breed would take a book by itself. Instead, let's take a brief look at some of the best known and some of the most unusual breeds. For your convenience, we've grouped them as longhairs, shorthairs, and orientals.

Longhairs

Sometimes looked upon as the pampered aristocrats of the feline world, longhaired cats require careful grooming by their owners. Most owners, however, will tell you that their cats are worth every single extra minute.

The Persian

Some say the Persian is the earliest of the longhaired cats and ancestor to them all. The Persian today can be found in more than 60 varieties and color variations. The Himalayan variety looks like a longhaired Siamese. The red Peke-Face variety is bred to look very much like a Pekingese dog. The delicate Chinchilla has a sparkling white coat that is lightly tipped at the edges with black in the face, ears, and along the back.

The Persian is probably the ancestor of all longhaired cats.

Persians are a small, cobby breed with large round eyes and a large head. Their placid nature and even disposition make them a popular candidate for apartment living. Busy, career-oriented owners, however, must remember that each Persian in the house will need about 15 minutes of grooming time each day!

The Maine Coon Cat

The first breed created in America was the Maine Coon, with a coat as rough and shaggy as its name. Maine Coons appeared in American cat shows as early as the middle of the 19th century. In 1895, a Maine Coon took Best-in-Show at Madison Square Garden.

One of the largest cat breeds, the Maine Coon was developed by crossings between Angora cats brought into the United States by British sailors and the semi-wild cats of the Maine forests and coastline. Although this cat does look like a raccoon, crossings with the raccoon are biologically impossible.

The Maine Coon cat was the first breed that originated in the United States.

An excellent hunter, the Maine Coon is equipped for survival. It has long legs and large paws that can be used almost like hands. But it is a gentle giant and a good family cat.

The Norwegian Forest Cat is similar to the Maine Coon in appearance and temperament, but it is a separate and very ancient breed.

The Turkish Van

White with spots of auburn color on the head and tail, the Turkish Van was discovered around the shores of Lake Van in Turkey. And guess what: They love to swim!

This is a sociable cat with a soft voice. The coat is semi-long (not nearly as long as the Persian), and the eyes are amber or blue. They'll do laps in the pool with you if you let them.

The Turkish Van loves to swim.

The Ragdoll

The Ragdoll is an all-American breed from the 1960s in California that is rarely seen outside North America. Probably the most laid-back of all cat breeds, Ragdolls will relax completely (they will actually go limp!) when picked up (hence their name) and will rarely fight for any cause. They are both nonaggressive and noncomplaining, and they are said to have so extraordinary a tolerance for pain that injuries can go unnoticed. Being so mild-mannered, they do better living indoors where they will have some protection.

The Ragdoll is among the most easygoing of breeds.

Ragdolls are large cats—as large as the Maine Coon—with semi-long fur and blue eyes that give more than a hint at their white Persian ancestry. Most experts believe there is also some Siamese in their background.

Shorthairs

Shorthaired cats far outnumber their longhaired cousins. Virtually all cats born in the wild are shorthaired because that gene is dominant. There is, however, great variety among cats with this coat characteristic.

The American Shorthair

The American Shorthair is the cat you are most likely to find on your doorstep. It's what most people visualize when they think of a cat. Of course, it is very similar to the breed from which it probably descended, the British Shorthair.

The oldest recorded coloring on the shorthair was the tabby, which is still both common and popular. Shorthairs also come in the solid colors: white, black, blue, cream, chocolate, and lilac. Or, if you prefer, you can choose tortoiseshell, calico, pointed, shaded, smoked, tipped, bi-colors, and vans. In other words, this is the most variety you're ever going to get in the cat world.

The American Shorthair has that all-American cat look.

The American Wirehair is exactly like its cousin except for a coat that got perhaps a little too much perm. It first appeared in Vernon, New York, in 1966.

The Scottish Fold

The Scottish Fold is an example of a spontaneous mutation. In 1961, on a farm in Perthshire, Scotland, a farm cat gave birth to a white kitten with folded ears. She was named Susie, and two years later she bore a kitten who looked very much like her.

The Scottish Fold is a cat with a teddy-bear face.

Further breeding showed that when Folds are bred to cats with normal ears, half the litter will be Folds. When Folds are bred to Folds, however, kittens may be born with a skeletal disorder where the vertebrae of the tail become fused and cartilage grows around the toes. It's important to remember, therefore, that this breed should always be mated with American, British, or Exotic Shorthairs, not with other Scottish Folds.

Folds are easygoing, loving, and intelligent cats with soft voices and tolerant dispositions. They do well in families.

The Chartreux

The Chartreux is a breed naturally occurring in France, where its dense, water-repellent blue fur is much admired.

With a large sturdy body and slender legs, it is both strong and agile, and is an excellent hunter.

This breed is sometimes confused with the blue-coated British Shorthair, but most American and French breeders keep the two breeds separate. The Chartreux is particularly loyal to its owner and its home. Many people believe the breed originated with the Carthusian monks in the 16th century.

The Chartreux has a lush, dense coat.

Orientals

Many new breeds have been derived by mating the ancient Siamese type cat with other purebreds. All have the lithe and graceful body type of their forebears.

The Siamese

The Siamese is the extrovert of the cat world. It greets everyone, demands its due attention, and expresses its opinion on everything. Some people are bothered by its rather loud voice, which it uses more or less constantly; others love the ongoing conversation.

The Siamese is a great talker.

Despite being a small, graceful, slender cat, the Siamese will usually dominate other cats in the household. Most Siamese love children and do well in family situations, even though they may consider one particular adult as their own. They are very intelligent and, like other aristocrats, can sometimes be moody.

The Abyssinian

Many people believe that the Abyssinian breed is the ancestor of all others, being the cat of ancient Egypt. It has a medium-sized body and long legs that combine with excellent musculature to produce the look of a fine athlete. The breed also has the energy of an athlete and needs space to exercise. Oh, and it loves to play in the water.

Abyssinians are intelligent, affectionate, and interact well with their owners. They will learn tricks and usually enjoy showing off and being praised. They do not like to be left alone for long periods of time, and they do not like to be crowded.

The Abyssinian is among the most active of all breeds.

The Oriental Longhair

Called the Oriental Longhair even though its coat is only semi-long, this breed combines many of the qualities of the Siamese and the Persian. It is thin and graceful but also strong and well muscled. The texture of its coat is fine and silky. The tail plume is especially long and feathery.

The Oriental Longhair usually gets along well with other pets in the family and with the family members, too. It's an especially curious and inquisitive cat and expresses its affections openly.

The Oriental Longhair has a Siamese body and a semi-long coat.

Your Moggie

The vast majority of cats in homes around the world have no pedigrees. You may be able to recognize traits in your cat's physical makeup or personality that align him or her with one of the established breeds, but you can't really prove anything. It doesn't matter. Your cat is an individual and precious as such—just like his or her human!

It's Been Said

"If man could be crossed with the cat, it would improve man but deteriorate the cat."

—Mark Twain

Chapter 8

Settling In, for Both of You

In This Chapter

➤ Cats are intelligent, although teaching them tricks can sometimes be...tricky

➤ Declawing: Is it necessary or just cruel?

➤ The many poisonous substances around your home

➤ Other household threats

Once your cat is more or less assimilated into your household—there might still be some hissing between the newcomer and your other pets—there are household decisions to make and actions to take.

For your first cat, you will have to look at your home as one big potential source of danger for your pet. That fluffball, whether she is a kitten or an eight-year-old, will no doubt be into *everything* as she explores her new turf.

Cats Can Be Taught a Thing or Two

Are cats intelligent? Well, *yours* is, of course, but what about all the others? Actually, it has been difficult to judge cats' smarts because it is hard to test them. They do not react well to the action/reward system of grading that scientists use with lab rats and mice. And while a dog will beg and perform tricks for praise or affection, few cats will so demean themselves or stand still long enough to be trained.

However, it is generally believed that cats are neither more nor less intelligent than other domesticated animals. Scientists working with cats note that they certainly can learn to respond to selected stimuli, and they show quite a bit of ingenuity. Of course, even without scientific tests, those of us who are owned by cats know they can indeed be very smart, clever, and even sly. And communicate? A cat expresses herself in many different ways—using her voice, her tail, her ears, the position of her body, and purring and licking her owner. All of that is "talking."

Those who have had their cat tear from an upstairs bedroom down to the kitchen in 10 seconds when it hears the can opener hit the tin of Tuna Treat will know that cats are quick-minded (they also have great hearing). There are cats that can open the refrigerator door as well as doors to outside the home (usually the latch kind that can be lifted).

A cat is apt to know its own name. Will it come when called? It might if it is so inclined. It can also learn perhaps 25 to 50 other words (dogs can learn a few more), most of them dear to its heart, such as "eat" and "treat." It will probably also respond to your own special terms of endearment, and its little ears pick up to "no," "stop," "stay," "down," and other reprimands, although it could be the stern tone of your voice that makes the cat obey.

What about tricks? Can you teach your cat to dance with a lampshade on her head? You can *try*. You might be able to train it to do simple tricks, such as sitting up and reaching for a treat or toy, with *much* repetition and with no session lasting more than 10 minutes, which is about the length of a cat's attention span. Your success will depend on the cat's intelligence and mood of the moment, along with the difficulty of the trick.

You are likely to have more luck teaching your pet no-nos, and scoring a few points in that area will make most owners happy enough. You can read more about this in Chapter 11.

Also in the brainy cat department is the question of how cats find their way home when lost or how they travel thousands of miles to rejoin an owner. Chapter 9 talks more about that phenomenon.

To Declaw or Not to Declaw

Here are the two schools of thought on this major issue: "He's going to be an indoor cat, but I don't want my furniture ruined, so I'm having him declawed," and "Declaw? Never. How would *you* like to have your nails pulled out one by one and be forced to walk around on stumps for the rest of your life?"

Which is the right way to go? It is don't declaw. In fact, these days many veterinarians will not perform that operation.

What about your home, you say? What about scratches to *you*?

Chapter 11 discusses ways of repelling your pet when it tries to sit on or scratch furniture, and Chapter 15 talks about the cat's reasons for doing this and other types of destructive behavior.

All of those suggestions mean a little more work for you, but they will bring the results you want without subjecting your pet to that loathsome operation.

Common Household Poisons

There are some products around your home that might as well carry a skull and crossbones on them as far as your pet is concerned. These include most cleaning agents, which should be kept out of reach. You might even want to invest in interior latches, sold at hardware stores, that keep kitchen, bathroom, and other cabinet doors from being opened by toddlers and curious cats.

Even drinking water from the toilet could cause your cat harm if you have cleaned the bowl with chemicals and their toxic residues remain in the water. It's best to keep the toilet lid down.

Keep the inquisitive one in another room when carpets are being cleaned and when fumigation is in progress. Also, be careful of products used on furniture to waterproof it or make it stain-resistant. Using aerosol sprays near a cat's food or water bowl can also cause it harm.

The problem isn't just their eating cleaning supplies and similar products, it is also their walking through those substances and then washing and licking it off themselves.

If your cat does somehow ingest a toxic substance, you will notice any one, or a few, of these symptoms:

- ➤ drooling
- ➤ respiratory difficulties
- ➤ vomiting
- ➤ fits
- ➤ staggering gait
- ➤ unconsciousness

Get the animal to a veterinarian without delay. Do not try homemade formulas, which could be toxic to pets or at the least waste valuable time. If a vet is some distance away, call and follow his or her directions for emergency treatment. You might also ask around at veterinary clinics and animal shelters for the number of a local poison control center, which might offer free advice.

If your pet seems to be in trouble from a toxic substance, you can also call the 24-hour National Animal Poison Control Center, a nonprofit service of the College of Veterinary Medicine at the University of Illinois. A veterinarian will answer the phone, or you will be connected to one. You can call (800) 548-2423 for a charge of $30 per case or (900) 680-0000 for $20 for the first five minutes and $2.95 for each additional minute. (The typical call lasts 10 minutes.) Your fee covers any follow-up calls. Payment is by credit card only.

The Greenery

Cats love to nibble on grass, which can be a good digestive aid. Their chewing on it can help them cough up a furball. However, an indoor cat, not likely to find a lawn in your living room, could start chomping on any green leaves it finds, such as plants on a tabletop or small trees on the floor.

The list of harmful house plants is a lengthy one. For example, avocado, dieffenbachia (also known as the mother-in-law plant or mother-in-law's tongue), English ivy, philodendron, the sturdy pothos, and the spider plant are bad for cats. So are the asparagus fern, Boston ivy, ficus (weeping fig), and shefflera.

If your cat goes outside, it might find other kinds of landscaping that could be bad for it. Cats should avoid azaleas, boxwood, buttercup, chrysanthemum, iris, laurel, lily of the valley, morning glory, oleander, poison ivy, and yew.

Ask your veterinarian whether he or she has a complete list of plants and flowers harmful to pets. You might inquire at a poison control center near you as well, or check with a local plant nursery.

"Good grief," you say, "Outdoors is one thing, but it sounds like I can't have *any* houseplants." But you can. For one thing, some cats never bother a plant. Yours could be one of them. Also, you can hang the toxic greenery up high or keep it out of a paw's reach. Try sprinkling cayenne pepper on the soil of your plants, the smell of which will repel your pet (you'll have to keep sprinkling though—the odor will fade and need to be refreshed). You can also grow catnip indoors for your pet to nibble on and to divert it from the bad stuff.

Safe plants for a cat to be around include begonias, coleus, dracaena, ferns, grape ivy, and several varieties of peperomia. Most cacti are safe, except for the pencil, peyote, and the candelabra cactus, which are poisonous.

Tabby Tips

If your cat likes to nibble a little salad, try growing a pot of grass just for kitty. Seeds for cat grass mixtures are available at many pet supply stores and through catalogs.

Besides chewing on plant leaves, cats will sometimes take up the unlovely habit of urinating in the pots. This is more likely with large-sized floor tubs, where they jump in, begin scratching the dirt, and water your plant for you. To discourage this habit, you might cover the dirt with cypress mulch or similar chips, loosely arranged playing marbles, or small pebbles, all of which disguise the smell of and access to the earth, while still allowing water and air through to the plant.

Jingle, Belle

As much as cats love Christmas—and some of them become adorably freaky when holiday decorations are brought out of storage—this holiday brings a new set of perils to the merry-making pet. Greenery that is either poisonous or otherwise dangerous to cats includes such favorites as holly, mistletoe, and even pine needles. In recent years, the poinsettia has been absolved of causing illness to cats, although you might still want to keep yours away from it as you would other plants.

Tinsel, angel hair (a synthetic substance that looks like a mop of golden hair and can be separated and placed in tree branches), glass ornaments, the hooks that hold ornaments to the tree, real berries, the water at the base of the tree (especially if you have added a chemical to it to prolong its life), and much of your Christmas tree are harmful to a pet. Try to place safe ornaments, such as small stuffed or wooden toys, on the lower part of the tree where the cat might be able to swat at them from the floor and get them into its mouth, and place the other decorations on higher branches. Either on the bottom or on the entire tree, substitute narrow ribbon for hooks.

Then there are the lights. Cover cords to outlets with wire camouflage so your cat cannot bite through them or stab them with its claws.

For the gymnastic feline, be sure the tree is anchored by wire, string, or a hook to some part of a wall or the ceiling in case it attempts to scale the tree and it topples. Actually, an artificial tree might not interest your cat at all and spare you some of the worry.

I'm so cute, I think I'll climb up the Christmas tree.

Keep an eye on your pet when exchanging gifts—this goes for all gift-giving occasions—so that it does not swallow the ribbon used for wrapping presents.

Whew, that's certainly a lot more work for you during an already busy time of year, isn't it? Still, all you need during those hectic days is an unexpected, frantic dash to the 24-hour veterinary clinic with a *very* sick cat. So it does pay to cat-proof your holiday decor along with your other furnishings.

Other Pussy Perils

How much mischief can a two-year-old toddler get into? Multiply that a few times and you will have some idea of where the curiosity of a cat, especially a kitten, can lead that pet. Using just the kitchen as an example, you will have to make sure there is no room for the cat to squeeze behind the refrigerator. Also watch that it does not get on top of the stove while it is lit. Cats love warmth and hidden places, so you will *always* have to check the clothes dryer before turning it on. Check the washing machine and even the dishwasher. When you have the refrigerator door open, glance inside before you shut it. It is amazing how quickly a kitten can leap into that appliance while your back is turned. When you think, "Where *is* that cat?" you will often be astonished at where the little whiskers turns up.

If you see your pet gnawing at electrical wires, you can buy wire camouflage strips at a hardware store. Naturally, you will want to keep the cat away from open windows and balconies.

Are you now feeling a little overwhelmed by all the threats to your cat from your home itself, plus its various plants, bottles, and powders? Are you wondering how you are going to keep one step ahead of your pet?

We have a suggestion that can help, especially if you are a first-time pet owner. Take a pad of Post-It notes, mark a number of sheets "cat," and stick them to the washing machine, clothes dryer, window ledges, cabinets under the kitchen and bathroom sinks, and all other sources of danger to your pet. Eventually, you will automatically think about the cat when you are near those appliances or parts of the house, and then you can remove the notes. After a while, being careful really does become second nature.

It's Been Said

"I love cats because I love my home; and little by little, they become its visible soul."

—Jean Cocteau

Chapter 9

Citizen Cat

In This Chapter

➤ Indoor versus outdoor cats

➤ Many communities have leash laws, even for cats

➤ When your pet is lost

Just as you have obligations beyond your front door as a citizen of your community, so too does your cat. Or let's say you do as *representative* for your cat. Although you might let your furball do almost anything it likes, your neighbors and the folks down at city hall are not likely to be so indulgent. You can read about minding your civic p's and q's in the next several pages.

Indoors or Out?

About two-thirds of all companion cats live exclusively inside. The remainder either go in and out or live outdoors

100 percent of the time. Check your community laws. Some prohibit "owned" cats from roaming freely.

What is the current buzz on the indoor/outdoor issue for pet owners who have a choice?

A cat *can* live a happy life indoors, and that is what professionals interested in cats' welfare are suggesting more and more these days. Sure, there are country cats, farm cats, and barn cats that can lead long lives outside, but there are many perils to life outdoors for other companion pets in built-up locales: traffic, other cats and animals, dangerous terrain, poisonous plants and food, and *people* who poison, torture, or kill cats. The typical cat living exclusively or mostly outdoors has an average life span of about three years. That's compared to 12 to 16 years or so for an indoor pet.

Dr. Franklin Loew, dean of Tufts University School of Veterinary Medicine, has said, "There are four keys to longevity in cats. One is luck; two is proper nutrition; three is health care, including appropriate vaccinations; and four is keeping out of harm's way." For most owners, harm's way is the great outdoors.

There is a compromise here: a controlled outdoor experience, where cats can feel the breeze on their fur, watch leaves fall at their feet, and even come precariously close to a bird or two. Some owners—with the space to do this, of course—rig up a shelter or a run made up of wood or wire fencing for their cat in the yard. Others keep their pets on a leash tied up out front or back so that they can experience the outdoors. Some take their cats for a stroll around the neighborhood. Really. We discuss more about the correct way to do this coming up.

There are also fencing systems that keep your cat confined to its own property when outdoors. Check cat magazines for advertisements for these products.

Finally, your community might just make the indoor/outdoor decision for you, as you will see in the next few pages.

Outdoor Safety

If you do decide to let your cat outside, keep these points in mind:

➤ It is best to keep cats indoors when the temperature plummets. Their fur coats are not that protective; they can suffer from hypothermia just like people.

➤ If your cat does go out, check its paw pads and between its nails regularly for salt and deicers. These products can irritate paws, and when they are ingested after the cat licks its feet clean, they can cause more trouble.

➤ Antifreeze has a sweet taste cats like, but even a few drops can be lethal. Make certain there are no puddles in your garage. You might want to switch to a *propylene* glycol instead of the highly toxic *ethylene* glycol-based product. One brand is Sierra; call (800) 289-7234 for local retailers. Another brand is Sta-Clean; call (800) 825-3464. The safer products will cost a little more than the other brands.

➤ When your car is parked outdoors, knock soundly on the hood before getting in and turning on the ignition. The knock should scare away any feline under the hood or the vehicle itself—two spots cats often head to for shelter from the cold.

The Pet Door

You have probably seen pet doors advertised as a major convenience, allowing your cat to go in and out of your home at will. The door comes in a variety of sizes and can be easily installed by a novice (making sure it is the right height for the cat to step through). A common style is a rubber flap that allows ease of movement with the cat going in and out and a slide that moves vertically up and down if you want to close the door at times. Some feature an indicator that tells you whether your cat is in or out, while others open only after matching a magnet that is on your pet's collar, which registers when that animal approaches, and lets it in. Cats without that magnetized collar cannot enter.

You can find pet door kits at hardware stores and home centers for around $30 to $70 or so, depending on the size you choose and the number of special features you elect. If the door you want will be between two inside rooms, you might want to skip the kit and create a less expensive entry of your own design with no need for a flap.

If you have a toddler around, you will want to make certain the opening isn't large enough for the child to squeeze through. Depending on your cat's smarts, it might take a while to train it to use the exit. One family who installed a pet door leading from the kitchen to the attached garage where they kept the cat litter was never able to train the cat to nose its way through. So they cut off the rubber entry flap, figuring the waste of heated/cooled air from the now-open pet door was minimal. The cat quickly learned to use the unblocked opening.

You will also want to make sure your pet door is far enough away from bolts and locks to deter burglars from inserting gadgets that can open your house door from the inside. Finally, you know that if your cat comes in after touring the neighborhood, so can other felines. Hmmm.

Some manufacturers offer products that are difficult to swing open, such as the door the cat pulls out when it is ready to come back in, making it impossible for a friend to follow it through without learning just how to do that. There is also the previously mentioned magnet that serves as a code to the door.

Local Pet Laws

In many communities, a cat, even one kept indoors, must be registered and licensed with the appropriate local government agency. There is, of course, an annual fee for that tag. Rabies inoculations are often required each year as well. Rabies, you say, for an *indoor* cat? Well, if your cat should accidentally slip out of the house, it will need that protection in the outdoors. Also, if a rabid bat or mouse or squirrel ever got into your place—not totally outside the realm of possibility—you would be glad your pet had that preventive shot.

Some towns do not allow "owned" cats to roam the streets unleashed any more than they do dogs that have a home.

Your local government can fill you in on leash and other pet laws in your area. If you violate a cat-at-large law, you might be charged a fine of anywhere from $15 to $1,000.

Sometimes you must answer to both your town and your residential community for a roaming cat. Many single-family homes, condominiums, and cooperative developments and mobile-home communities have bylaws that state, among other dos and don'ts, that there can be no more than a specific number of pets per household and that they are allowed out only on a leash. If you are considering moving, be certain to ask your real estate agent or the seller of the home you are considering buying to show you the bylaws *before* you make a deposit on any property. Although the laws can be changed during your residency in those communities, you will have input about changes then.

Restrictions can also apply to those in rental apartments. Some buildings or complexes allow pets; others do not or limit their number per household.

An exception to the no pets rule is federally funded developments designated exclusively for renters who are disabled or elderly.

Pet restrictions can be a complicated area. Usually, if you sign a lease with a no-pets clause, you must not have, or subsequently acquire, companion animals. However, at least one exception is New York City, where there is an ordinance prohibiting landlords from enforcing the no-pets rule if a tenant has lived openly with his or her animal for three months or more.

If you have a problem or questions in this area, you can call the Animal Legal Defense Fund at (415) 459-0885 for information or the name of an attorney in your community knowledgeable about this legal specialty.

Walking Matilda

Of course you can walk your cat. It isn't only dogs that are permitted to enjoy a stroll around the neighborhood. In fact, as mentioned earlier, you might live in a community where your cat is allowed out only on a leash, so you will dutifully *have* to walk it if it likes to get beyond your property line.

When starting this adventure, you might want a harness and lead for the animal so that it will not escape at the first sight of an alluring bird. This is better for a cat than a leash attached to its collar. Let the cat wear the harness a bit around the house so that it becomes used to it before going out.

Your cat is...well, a cat, and not Fido. When it is outside, it will not walk in a straight line but will wander this way and that, sniffing and investigating sights and sounds.

That's okay. Being a good citizen, you will not, of course, allow your pet to chew the geranium beds of the folks down the street. You might want to keep the cat off lawns in the summertime, too. Some may have been treated with dangerous chemicals.

The ambling cat could well pick up fleas, although you don't need an outside cat for an infestation in your home. It's wise to keep a close eye on your pet for any manifestation of that serious cat—and household—problem.

Some cats are eager to go for a stroll, others quite definitely are not. If yours seems to fight the harness, or going outside at all for that matter, drop the whole business. The cat can, as mentioned elsewhere in these pages, live quite happily indoors.

If Your Cat Is Lost

You might want to reread the section of Chapter 3 that discusses placing identification on your pet in the event it becomes lost, which can happen even if yours is an indoor cat. For example, if you hold your front door open a second too long, the cat might dash out before anyone can catch it.

If you lose your pet and you live in a community with leash laws even for cats, your pet could have been picked up and transported to the local animal shelter. You might have to pay a fine to retrieve it. As Chapter 3 brings up, you have several identification choices for your cat. It's wise to choose one as soon as you bring the animal home. Although none of them guarantees its return, identification certainly helps.

Less than 5 percent of lost cats brought to animal shelters ever find their way back home to their owners, so you will have to work to see the return of your pet. First, of course, search your home. Are you surprised at that rather obvious suggestion? Those of you who have searched for your cat for 10 hours, frantic and teary-eyed, convinced it was gone forever, only to have it turn up sleeping in the back of a bureau drawer you had opened that morning, will know the wisdom of that suggestion. Searching means everywhere, not just the cat's hangouts. Obviously, it is somewhere else, so look where you would never expect to find it.

Then search your neighborhood, even ringing neighbors' doorbells and asking about your AWOL pet.

If you still have no luck, drive slowly around your community, getting out of the car at times to hunt on foot. You might bring a box of cat food with you to rattle and lure your cat out if it is hiding.

If the cat is identified by a microchip or a tag listed with a central directory, you will want to follow the directions for a lost pet issued with those items.

You can phone area animal shelters to see if they have your cat. Call them frequently because if the animal eventually shows up there, you will have to rescue it pretty quickly before it is offered for adoption or is euthanized.

Draw up a flyer with a picture if possible, a description of the animal, and the location where it was last seen. You might also note if you are offering a reward for its return. Close with your name and/or phone number. Put the flyers on bulletin boards at nearby stores, places of worship, schools, and anywhere else where a person who might find your pet will look.

You also could have some success with an advertisement in your local newspaper's classified columns under "Pets Lost." If you have a daily paper and a weekly neighborhood publication, try both.

The Radar That (Sometimes) Gets Them Home

What about those television news features and newspaper accounts about cats that followed their owners 2,000 miles from their old home to their new home, crossing unfamiliar, rugged terrain but arriving in one piece at the astonished owner's door weeks, even months, after their parting? Could your lost cat find its way back from that distance? How do they *do* that, anyhow?

No one is exactly sure how pets perform this feat. The reasons remain the cats' own, but the subject does tantalize those conducting studies. Some say the cats use the sun as a guide; others point to the animals' excellent sensory perception.

Two German scientists performed an interesting experiment. They took some cats on a drive around their city, weaving in and out of streets to throw off the cats' sense of direction. Then they returned to their lab where the cats were put in a large maze with several exits, all of them facing different directions. The overwhelming majority of cats chose the exit that lay closest to their home.

How *did* they do that?

The Classic Tree Problem

Help! Your cat is up a tree. What can you do? You are supposed to let it make its way back down, the theory being if it could climb up, it can reverse the process. A cat's claws curve downward, though, making the ascent easy. Returning, it has to back down out of the tree. Waiting for a cat to figure this out is when most folks panic and call the local fire department. Try setting an open can of cat tuna (strong-smelling to attract your pet) on the highest branch you can reach and then wait for the explorer to descend.

It's Been Said

"Cats in general have always had as their chief assignment our aesthetic satisfaction."

—Roger Caras

Chapter 10

Mealtime—High Point of a Cat's Day

In This Chapter

➤ A regular feeding schedule and a regular dining spot

➤ Nutritionally balanced commercial food

➤ Do cats need vitamins?

➤ About special treats

The sound of a can opener grinding through the lid of a tin can or the rattle of a box or bag of cat food at certain times of the day are sweet music to a feline.

Food is of major interest to all cats, but especially to those that live indoors and focus their days around dining. That's fine. We have much to choose from in pet food these days that's delicious (we're assuming) and nutritious (we know), so there's no reason for your furry friend to become bored with the menu. And there's certainly no reason for it to be malnourished.

Isn't That Special

Just as we have *our* eating hangouts at home, most cats like to know they can find their meals in their own spot, in the same place, when the dinner bell sounds.

The spot should be out of the path of household traffic and near no offensive odors. Certainly, it ought to be a good distance from the litter box.

The "table setting" will include a food dish and a water bowl with fresh water poured several times a day. The latter is a nutritional necessity. A cat might lose up to 50 percent of its overall weight and survive. But if it loses just 15 percent of its water weight, it will die.

Most folks feed their cat twice a day, a morning meal and another meal in the late afternoon or early evening. Some spread that food across three meals. Try to stick to a schedule. No doubt your cat will give you a hand by wailing when mealtime is near.

In some households with a dog and a cat, the dog eats the cat's food as well as its own. You can move the cat's food up to the kitchen counter where the cat can jump to eat it but the dog can't. If you are in a house of a certain style, you can keep the door to a garage, cellar, or pantry closed, put in a pet door big enough for the cat but not the dog, and put the cat's food in that area. In a multi-cat household with cats on different diets, it's possible to buy a pet dish rigged for just one cat (the bowl has a matching collar for the cats you want to keep out of that bowl, which emits a tone to the cats to discourage them from eating from that dish). Look for ads in cat magazines and catalogs to find this type of dish.

The Pet Food Selection

Cats are carnivores. They must eat meat. Most of the popular commercially prepared cat food available contains all the nutrients your pet needs—protein, fat, vitamins, and minerals. In fact, our furry friends are eating more balanced meals than many of their owners!

The reputable pet food companies are constantly experimenting with the content and taste of their foods. This is a huge business, as you might have noted from the length of the pet food aisle at the supermarket. In the United States, cat food sales *doubled* during the 1980s to reach *$2 billion a year*—more than the amount spent for baby food.

Incidentally, cat food is one of those products where you really do get what you pay for. The most expensive foods tend to be better nutrition-wise. And the cost is really deceptive, anyway, because with the better foods, you usually feed the cat less. Since less food goes in, you'll also find less coming out in the litter box—an added bonus.

Cats prefer their food at room temperature. Moist food can stand out 30 minutes or so, but then it should be taken away and the uneaten portion should be scraped into the garbage. Cats like to nibble, go away, come back for more nibbles, and so on. But canned food can become quite unappetizing if left uneaten all day, not to mention potentially dangerous in warm weather. Some owners have a small bowl of dried food always available to their pet so it can munch round-the-clock.

But much as they like it, free-feeding is not right for every cat. If your pussy is getting a bit pudgy, it's best to keep it on a regular feeding schedule. Put its food down for half an hour, and then pick up the bowl whether it's empty or not. If you must let a chubby cat munch all day, carefully measure the amount and make sure it doesn't get any extras.

Tabby Tips

If your cat is ill, it's important to know whether or not it is eating. Regular mealtimes will help you monitor its appetite.

When it comes to the question of wet, semi-moist, or dry, most veterinarians recommend dry. It's better for the cat's teeth, and ounce for ounce, dry food has a lot more nutrition packed into it. If you'd like to feed your cat wet food, make it just a small part of its diet and feed it mainly dry. The semi-moist foods are loaded with sugar and artificial colors and flavors, which your cat does not need.

Health Diets

In recent years, many pet food companies have focused on specialized markets, coming out with meals for kittens, for seniors, and for the pudgy cat. Some manufacturers have also developed products to help prevent LUTD (lower urinary tract disease), sometimes called FUS (feline urinary syndrome). Besides LUTD, there are other health problems where symptoms can be alleviated to some extent with specialized diets. Talk with your vet about any special foods, some of which can be found easily at the supermarket.

Never switch to a new diet for health reasons without first checking with your vet. If you do get the green light, introduce the new food in what your cat is now eating a little at a time, gradually easing out of the old diet. Starting out overnight with totally different meals can cause gastrointestinal upsets to your pet.

Although your cat is likely to show some preferences for certain flavors of cat food, don't let it narrow its meals to one choice. Eating just liver, for example, is not good. Feeding it only fish could cause a Vitamin B deficiency.

Giving your cat prepared *dog* food, which might be tempting if you have a dog in the house, is a definite no. Their meals are not interchangeable. The meat content in prepared dog foods is not high enough for cats, and certain amino acids and important vitamins are missing.

In 1978, scientists discovered that taurine, a colorless amino acid, was essential in a feline's diet to prevent eye problems leading to blindness. Pet food companies responded to this news by adding that ingredient to their cat foods. In 1986, a link was found between a lack of taurine and heart disease in cats. The amount of taurine in cat food at the time was not enough, so manufacturers raised the level. Taurine is not included in dog food ingredients because dogs have no need for it.

Tabby Tips

Some owners prefer homemade food for their cats. Be sure to check with your veterinarian before introducing such a diet, however, because you will have to be careful that your pet is receiving all the protein, vitamins, and minerals it needs. You also might want to read *The New Natural Cat* by Anitra Frazier with Norma Eckroate (Plume) or *Dr. Pitcairn's Complete Guide to Natural Health for Dogs and Cats* by Richard H. Pitcairn and Susan H. Pitcairn (Rodale Press).

About Vitamins

Thanks to complete prepared commercial foods, cats do
not need special vitamin supplements.

Veterinarians say they see more health problems with pets
suffering from vitamin excesses, or toxicities, than those
related to vitamin deficiency. Keep in mind that if your
cat food contains at least the required amount of a
vitamin—and some foods contain several times that
dose—giving your cat still more vitamins could harm it.

Table Scraps and Other Treats

The tendency to feed one's pet some food from the table
starts early in many households. After all, if we find that
roast turkey absolutely delicious, why not pass that enjoyment on to the cat?

First of all, it should be pointed out that some cats have
no interest at all in human food. If they do, from your
occasional treat can grow a habit that becomes difficult to
break as your cat rushes to the kitchen each time you do,
hoping for any snack from leftover meatloaf to canta-
loupe. Occasional bits from the table are not likely to
harm most cats, but those snacks shouldn't be a regular
occurrence. If it is eating commercial cat food, your pet
does not need the food *you* eat. You might discover that:

➤ The cat finds some of it indigestible.

➤ Too many nibbles combined with the regular pet
  food meals it is scarfing down have piled on the
  pounds.

➤ It is becoming a fussy eater, preferring the table
  scraps to cat food.

It can be dangerous for your cat's health, and it is certainly nutritionally inadequate, to feed it raw meat.

Never put your cat on a vegetarian diet either. Cats are carnivores, and you must respect that. Cooked chicken or turkey is a feline favorite, but be certain that what you set out has no bones. Besides being boned, fish must be carefully cut up and should never be served raw. Avoid giving tuna fish for humans to your cat; stick to cat tuna. Break the food you serve into small pieces. Some cats have a hard time digesting milk or cream, but surprise—they don't need either.

Finally, if you give your pet people meals *instead* of cat food, it may eventually suffer from malnutrition! Your food will not constitute the balanced chow a cat needs.

Nibbles sold commercially as cat treats should be handled as just that—a treat and not a dessert after every meal. They are not formulated to be complete meals—just tasty extras from time to time. And don't make the mistake one owner did, until she was filled in by a friend, and shake out a whole package of treats into the cat's food bowl as dinner!

Feeding the Overweight Cat

Your cat *looks* like a couch potato, but she isn't sprawled on the sofa watching television and downing chips and brewskies (well, maybe she *does* spend a good deal of time on the sofa). How did she pile on those extra pounds? The same way we do—eating more than we can work off with exercise. (By the way, there is no reason to expect that a spayed or neutered cat will automatically gain weight.)

You might want to have your pet checked by the veterinarian to be certain its thyroid gland is functioning properly, which could be a medical reason for weight gain. If everything is fine there, you can talk with your vet about knocking off some of those pounds. Obesity in cats can lead to arthritis and diabetes.

Tabby Tips

Cats lose weight the same way we do: eating less and exercising more. You might try engaging your chubby cat in more activity.

Some pet food companies have brought out "lite" lines for the chubby kitty. You might ask your vet about them. Although it is difficult to tell just how lite the manufacturer means because calorie counts are not required on labels, you can call the pet food company for more information (the phone numbers are on the inside back cover).

The Finicky Cat

"He's a very finicky eater. But then, aren't all cats a little fussy?" Nooooo, they're not. Most owners who say this have a spoiled cat rather than a delicate eater. Yes, spoiled.

There are all sorts of reasons cats start to turn up their noses at certain foods, but most date to our seemingly harmless efforts to offer our pets ever more delicious meals. The animal then becomes so selective it has us jumping through hoops trying to please it.

What can you do with a fussy eater? Steel yourself to ignore its meowing when you put down food you know it has eaten before and apparently enjoyed. Don't reach for something new to appease it. Leave that dish out for 15 minutes. If the fluffball hasn't eaten it, pick it up and take it away. Put down the same kind of food for the next meal. If the cat still won't bite, feed it a small amount of its favorite meal, but not enough to satisfy it. Keep up that feeding program until Mr. Particular learns that refusing one dish is not going to lead to something better.

A few cats are truly finicky, but their number is small. Some pedigreed cats fall into this category. If a cat has had poor eating habits since kittenhood and must be coaxed to eat—even if its heart desire is not the best, most nutritious food—then that is what you will have to do to keep it from starving. In most cases, however, the cat has just been cleverly manipulating its owner.

The Aging Cat's Nutritional Needs

Like older people, older cats sometimes eat less and seem to want familiar, favorite dishes. Tuna is one preference, perhaps because of its strong smell, which manages to reach a cat's fading senses.

Your veterinarian can help you decide what's best for your old cat, taking into account health problems it may have developed in its later years and the fact that its protein requirement is likely to be different from what it was during its growth and reproductive years. Perhaps a special diet from one of the commercial food companies making special products for "seniors" will fill the bill perfectly at this time in your cat's life.

It's Been Said

"Cats are rather delicate creatures and they are subject to a good many ailments, but I never heard of one who suffered from insomnia."

—Joseph Wood Krutch

Chapter 11

Good Housekeeping

SCRATCH
SCRATCH...

In This Chapter

➤ The fur flies—everywhere

➤ The benefits of a scratching post

➤ Pet stains

➤ Training your cat

He's here, he's there, he's everywhere, that cat. Can you have a relatively tidy, attractive home in spite of the cat?

Of course you can, with some thought and preparation. What we'll talk about here are practical tips for maintenance, repair, and decorating, keeping in mind that in homes with pets, there *will* be traces of the little dears here and there. After all, it's their home too. Cat owners understand that. Most will be happy just keeping it all under control.

Will the Cat's Bed Be the Same as Yours?

Many owners do not want their pets to sleep on the bed with them at night or indeed to jump on the bed at any time. Cats can be trained, through repetition and other suggestions in this chapter, to stay off the bed. They usually have the whole house or apartment to search for a place—or two or three—to snooze during the three quarters or so of the day that they sleep, so don't feel you are being too severe shooing them off the bed.

Then there are those who delight in having their pet beside them, head on the pillow or snuggled under the covers, at bedtime. The music these owners fall asleep to is the soft purr of a contented pet. Unfortunately, what they often wake up to—and too early at that—is that pet sitting on the owner's head, licking her face, or reaching out with its paws and claws to wake up the sleepy head. There's some accommodating to do by both parties if you let your cat on the bed. Many a cat's slumber has been disturbed by an owner's restless tossing.

Official Cat Beds

You might want to buy a cat bed to keep your pet's snoozing quarters separate from your own. Prices range from about $15 on up to over $100.

Whatever style you choose, a cat bed should be washable or at least have a washable mat or cushion. It ought to be made of fire-retardant materials, too. Plastic is best for not harboring the dreaded fleas, but make sure you pad that plastic with a comfy pillow.

Giving cats their own place to sleep should keep them from the digging they do with their claws when they are about to settle down, kneading that could harm bed linens or living-room upholstery if a pet chooses those spots for a nap.

About That Litter Box

Cats are the perfect pets because you don't have to walk them. They just use the litter box.

Oh yes, that litter box—filling it, cleaning it, and first of all, of course, deciding where it should go around your place.

Most folks opt for an out-of-the-way spot, naturally, both for their sake and the cat's. Cats do like their privacy when heading for the litter box. The chosen area is usually an extra bathroom, the garage, the basement, or the porch. In some homes, alas, there are few choices. A small apartment, for example, may have just one bathroom. The owner can keep the box under the sink if there is no cabinet, sewing two pieces of fabric around a strip of elastic and making a "skirt" to put around the sink. The cat can go through the curtain-like opening where the material meets. If there is no space under the sink, owners are often forced to keep the litter box elsewhere in the bathroom, and never mind that it won't be out of sight.

Here's another idea: If you have no space ideally suited for a litter box, put it in the corner of a living room or a spare room with an inexpensive decorative screen around it, hiding it from view. These are available commercially.

You can try a covered litter box, which certainly keeps the filler from spilling, but your success will depend on whether your cat is receptive to that concept. And whether it will *fit* into that closed space. Some bruisers don't.

Of course, no matter where you put the box, and no matter what type of litter you choose, you *must* scoop every day. Pussy will thank you. Your nose will thank you. Your guests will thank you.

Hair! It's Everywhere

Little balls of fur move, like tumbleweed, across your bare
wood floors at the slightest puff of air. Cat hair clings to
your carpets. And look at the sofa and club chair (assuming your cat is allowed on them). You can almost see
pussy's outline in left-behind fur on the spot it favors for
its naps.

Cat hair can be both sticky—adhering to some surfaces—
and elusive, as it flies away from others while you are trying to clean it up. You can keep it to a minimum by regularly brushing your pet, but you'll still have to clean.

An upright vacuum cleaner is likely to do a better job on
your rugs than the canister type. It goes deeper into the
pile. It's better for flea control, too.

Frequently sweeping bare wood floors might be followed
by a quick once-over with a wet mop if the surface has a
sturdy coat or two of polyurethane so that you aren't
washing untreated wood. Some folks vacuum wood floors,
which is fine if you can do it without scratching the
wood.

It is possible to vacuum upholstery too, of course, but for
quick fixes for hair on sofas, chairs, and beds, run a damp
cloth over those spots.

You can also buy products that will pick up fur. One company, 3M, puts out something called Pat-it, a sticky sheet
of pet hair remover that can also be used for lint. Just dab
it on the furniture's furry spots.

Maybe you don't have to buy anything at all. Check your
kitchen drawers for a rubber jar opener. Rub that on the
hairy surface, in one direction, and it'll pick up enough
fur to make another cat. It's cheap too, around $1 or so if
you have to spring for one. You can often find these
household aids in the supermarket around shelves of food
in jars.

Tabby Tips

The cleaning product that won the 1995 best of year in *Cat Fancy* magazine is called *FURniture Magnet*, from the company of the same name. It wipes hair off furniture and can be washed and re-used. Call (800) 738-4247 or (800) PET-HAIR for more information.

Scratching Posts, Wanted and Unwanted

R-i-i-i-i-p. Is there a sound more bloodcurdling to a cat owner than hearing her cat tear upholstery? Scratching bare wood, especially if it is Granny's heirloom rocker or something equally valuable, is probably almost as dismaying. Scratching at—even climbing—draperies also makes the blood run cold (an alternate window covering might be blinds, shades, or valances).

Cats have a very real need to scratch. They have scent glands in their feet, and when they scratch, they not only sharpen their claws and shed old, loose nails, but also mark their scent. Finally, cats scratch to stretch their back. Scolding them for doing what comes naturally will only confuse them.

You need a scratching post so that your cat can be happy clawing and you can be happy at what it's *not* tearing. (You need to have your pet's nails clipped regularly, too.)

A scratching post is just that—a chunk of wood or other sturdy material covered by a rug (use the underside because its good side will send your cat the message that it's all right to claw at carpets), sisal rope, burlap, corrugated cardboard, or some equally sturdy fabric appealing to a cat. Its only purpose is to provide the animal with an out-let for scratching and stretching. It ought to be at least three feet tall—as tall as your pet when it stands up on its hind legs, so it can get a good stretch. It must also be anchored so that the cat can't tip it over. What you are simulating here is a cat scratching at tree bark.

You can buy a scratching post or you can make one. Set it down near your cat's bed so it can exercise its need to stretch out and claw at something when it wakes from sleep.

What Cats Don't Like to Scratch

You need to make the objects your cat likes to scratch—and which you don't want it to—unappealing.

Take a sheet of contact paper, sticky side up, or two-sided tape, and run it along where you *don't* want your cat, tack-ing the ends to keep it firm. When it jumps up, it won't stay *there* long. Or you can use aluminum foil, which makes a crinkly, tinny sound your cat also won't like.

Or take a can filled with coins or pebbles and a piece of string tied to the can. Tack or tape the string across the scratching area. When the cat scratches, the can will fall near it and the noise will startle it. The cat is not likely to go back there. Keep your traps in effect a week or two after your cat stops attacking those items, just to be sure your plan is working.

Spraying the animal with a water spritzer can also be effective. However, it must be done as you catch it in the act, and you won't always be there then. It can be a good backup when you *are* around, though.

There are citrus and menthol-based sprays sold for this purpose—odors your cat will find offensive but which won't harm your furniture. Check cat magazines and your vet's office for items advertised or sold there. Eucalyptus oil is also a turn-off to cats. You can try sprinkling a little on threatened upholstery.

While you are saying "hands off" to some things, you should at the same time be guiding your cat to the scratching post (you might need two if your home is large), where you are offering it an okay alternative to its first choices.

You might smear the surface of the post with catnip to make it even more alluring. Guide its paws over the post in a scratching motion. You can put some of its toys near there and play there with it. Regularly place a treat at the top of the post, and praise your pet lavishly each time you see it clawing away. Of course, all of this training will take some time and patience.

There is a relatively new product in the war against scratching: soft vinyl claw caps that are glued onto your cat's nails and replaced every month or two as the nail is shed. The cat doesn't mind the caps and can still scratch, only now its nails are blunt with a plastic coating and not liable to do harm. The nails are advertised in cat magazines, available at veterinary clinics, pet supply stores, and through mail-order catalogs. Your vet can put them on your pet, although as you watch you might learn and do it yourself next time.

Scratch-Proof Decorating

If it's your style, you can decorate with leather or Naugahyde, neither of which seem to interest most cats. They prefer nubby to smooth surfaces. They might want to nap on such a sofa but not scratch it. Other smooth surfaces that don't hold much interest for them are marble and lacquer-finished pieces.

Cats might scratch wicker furniture, but it takes a long time for those claw marks to become visible, and they can often be easily covered by light sanding and repainting those spots.

When it comes to fabric, felines prefer (meaning they like to scratch) material with some substance for them to dig into with their nails. For example, they don't care much for chintz (polished cotton) because it's too smooth. However, tweeds and other rough textures are perfect.

Rugs—Out Damn Spot

Even a house or apartment with hardwood floors will have an occasional area rug. Have you noticed how cats love to play with an area rug? Oh, you have.

Maybe your cat moves it around until it's clear across the room and rolled up a bit. You might want to buy undercarpeting or tape that is sold with the purpose of keeping an area rug in the area you've chosen for it.

In a home with a cat or two, area rugs and wood floors are much easier to keep clean than wall-to-wall carpeting. Flea control is easier too (they love to burrow into wall-to-wall carpets), although fleas can also head for cracks and crevices in wood floors.

Tabby Tips

Heloise, the newspaper columnist, offers *Heloise's Cat-Care Hints* for $2. Send a self-addressed, stamped (55 cents) envelope to Heloise/Cat, P.O. Box 795001, San Antonio, TX 78279.

Now, about "accidents" on rugs. They will happen, and you are likely to eventually find yourself with several products from the supermarket or veterinary clinic that can be used for cleaning. Which is best? Each owner has a favorite. You will probably have to conduct some home tests to see what works on your particular carpet. Some liquids or sprays might leave more problems than they take away—widening a stain, for example, or discoloring that patch of rug.

Cleaning urine from a floor can be especially important because you don't want your cat returning to that area and making it a secondary litter box. You also don't want your home to smell. Use paper towels to get up as much liquid as possible. Then rinse with water. Blot the area with paper towels, then rinse with distilled white vinegar (which can also be used on upholstered furniture). Let it air dry.

If there is still an odor when the spot is dry, cover it generously with baking soda and leave it for several days, covered with a sheet of plastic if your cat has used the area often. Clean up the baking soda with a dust pan and brush, not a vacuum cleaner, which can be harmed by the powder.

It's Been Said

"No animal should ever jump upon the dining room furniture unless absolutely certain he can hold his own in the conversation."

—Fran Lebowitz

Chapter 12

Fun and Games

In This Chapter

➤ Exercise and playtime

➤ Inexpensive toys found around your home

➤ The delights of catnip

All cats are different in breed and in temperament. But they do have a few important things in common: They need exercise, they like to play, and they like—*love*—their owners.

Put all of that together, add some inspiration on your part when it comes to fun and games, and you wind up with many enjoyable moments spent with your pet. Call it quality time. Call it bonding. The result is a closer, happier relationship on both sides and as much understanding as possible between the two of you.

Cats and Exercise

Cats need regular exercise or movement, from kittenhood to old age, just the way humans do to stay in fit condition. If you can spend 15 minutes a day with your pet, getting it to move around or playing with it, you'll have a healthier, happier feline on your hands.

First, a point that applies to all the suggestions in this chapter: As you know, there are shy cats and outgoing ones, cats that play well with other cats, and those that seem to prefer human companionship. Of course, you'll want to gear your play activities toward your own pet's temperament and preferences.

A game many cats love that is excellent exercise is tossing a ball, or even paper scrunched up to form a ball, and letting your pet run to it. Expecting it to bring the object back to you might be asking a bit too much. Unlike dogs, cats do not seem to know almost instinctively to bring the ball back to you so you can throw it again. You might be able to train your pet to bring it back by using patience and rewards it considers pleasurable—attention and praise from you or a kitty treat.

A growing number of owners are taking their indoor cats out for walks, using a harness. The cat gets outside in a controlled environment and gets to move those furry little legs. The owner gets some exercise, too. For more about cat walks, see Chapter 9.

Inexpensive or Free Fun

Cats love to hide. Paper bags provide a fascinating diversion, as do cartons. Some cats love it if, when they've hopped inside a box, you fold over the flaps so they are completely hidden for a while.

Tie almost anything—bird feathers, a cork, an empty spool of thread, a pine cone—to a piece of string, elastic, or wire and swirl it around for your cat to catch. You can also fasten the contraption to a door handle so it swings free for the cat to swat.

Many cats love playing under the bed covers. You can box with your pet when it's beneath the comforter and you're not, without having to worry about scratches. When you change linens, you are likely to find your cat smack in the middle of the bed, waiting for you to make the new sheets billow, which seems to delight many adult cats, not to mention kittens, as they run around the top of the bed.

Some cats are fascinated by wind-up toys such as a toddler's very small car or truck. Others are wide-eyed at bubbles you blow in the air in their direction, which you can buy for about $2 in a store's toy department.

Tabby Tips

51 Ways to Entertain Your House Cat While You're Out by Stephanie Laland (Avon Books, $7.50) offers tips with illustrations for low- or no-cost playthings to keep kitty amused. Here's one: Put a few walnuts (in their shells, of course) in an empty tissue box and tape over the opening. Cut a paw-sized hole in the side of the box and rattle the box in front of your cat. He may spend hours scratching at the box and moving it around trying to get all the walnuts out.

There are a few cautions here. Be sure your toy, home-made or store bought, does not have detachable parts your cat can chew off and ingest or is not so small that the animal can swallow the whole thing in one gulp.

Be very careful about offering your pet any length of string, yarn, or ribbon. Many an owner has made a fast trip to the veterinary clinic after the cat has swallowed a mouthful of one of those substances. They can cause serious intestinal damage.

One of the simplest, and probably most popular, diversions for your pet is the windowsill. Cats can sit for hours watching what's passing and dozing off. They will make those strange cackling sounds at birds they see, track falling leaves, and, most important for an indoor pet, feel the warmth of the sun. Many cat people make sure any home they move into has windowsills wide enough to accommodate their cat!

If your home does not have a wide windowsill, you can purchase what is advertised in cat magazines as cat perches or shelves, which can be hooked onto a windowsill to give a cat a comfortably covered spot from which to look outside. They cost around $35.

If You Have Money to Spend

If you have a front or back yard, you might want to put in a birdhouse or bird bath to keep your indoor cat entertained. A bird feeder will hold its interest, too and can be affixed to an exterior wall of a house or apartment or on a fire escape.

Consult gardening books to see what you can plant that will attract butterflies to your garden, which will entrance your cat when it's sitting on the windowsill.

You can get pretty fancy for your pet. Kitty condos, or gyms, costing anywhere from $50 to $200 or so, usually consist of a several-foot-high building with entrances and ledges where your cat can climb and perch. They are available at pet supply stores and through mail-order catalogs.

If there's a handy person in the family, he or she might construct some stairs just wide enough for the cat against the side of a wall leading straight up and ending near the ceiling. Cats love height. Yours can spend hours on the top stair surveying its realm below. Some do-it-yourselfers erect a catwalk across a kitchen or living room ceiling that can fit in nicely with the decor as a sort of decorative beam. Add a spot in the room for the cat to get up to that plywood plank and down again on the other side.

The Pleasures of Massage

One of the most relaxing things you can do with your cat, while still accomplishing something, is the massage. You can almost feel your blood pressure drop as you rub your little friend, and you can see and feel the cat relax. Ahhhh—for both of you.

You can conduct a cat massage standing up, sitting, kneeling (perhaps on a rug or your bed), lying down with the cat beside you, or even standing with the cat on a high table like a human massage.

You most likely know how and where your cat likes to be petted and scratched. Now focus that attention on all of it, from gently rubbing your thumb on its forehead to an equally gentle running of your hand along its tail.

Your cat will most likely roll over and stretch during all of this, or perhaps fall quietly asleep. Some cats, post-massage, will jump up, raring to go.

The cat massage serves a few purposes. Besides being relaxing for both of you, moving your hands along your cat's body will allow you to check for irregularities, such as lumps, so that you can have the animal checked by your vet as soon as you notice any changes. If the animal cries when you touch a certain spot, that's another signal to call the vet. Finally, you can also look for fleas and other pests while you are kneading away.

Cat Language

Here are two French terms to help with your massage: **Cat effleurage** is a series of gentle strokes, moving downward with both your hands, one on each side of the spine. **Cat petrissage** is gently kneading your pet, exerting slight pressure from your thumbs.

Some points to watch: Your cat could easily become over-stimulated at some point during a massage and begin scratching or biting or just scurry off. It's time to stop then. Also, don't massage your cat when it is ill, although it is tempting to think that a nice rub will help it feel better.

Whee, Catnip!

Massage and now catnip. Oh, to be reincarnated as one of our own cats, right?

Just one whiff of this unique herb sends most cats into a reaction that humans might call ecstasy. The cat rolls over, purrs, growls, and sometimes leaps into the air. Some become aggressive and bop a fellow house cat on the noggin. Interestingly, catnip has both a stimulating and a relaxing effect on them, although cat reactions vary. A small minority of cats get no bang at all from catnip, although they might eagerly munch on its leaves.

What *is* that stuff anyway?

Catnip is a member of the mint family, related to more familiar kitchen herbs such as sage and thyme. It used to be a common plant in herb gardens and was once the base for a quite popular beverage in England—dried catnip leaves in boiling water. The tea was said to have a calming effect. It's a rare person today who brews a cup of catnip tea for himself after putting some of the herb out for his cat, but if you like, you certainly *can*.

The chemical that gives your cat a buzz is called nepetalactone, which is set into action by smell and then works on the cat's nervous system. It is safe and non-addictive.

Because it distracts a cat and does have that soothing effect, you might want to give your cat a little catnip before it must travel, when you are busy moving, or at any other time of stress (perhaps those are times for a nice cup of catnip tea for *you!*).

However, like anything special, it should not be available 24 hours a day. Put it out for a while, then take it away for a few days. You don't want your cat always hyped or in a perpetually lethargic state. Catnip should not be given to a cat going outdoors either, because the animal might be unable to care for itself while under its influence.

Because the scent eventually fades, every once in a while you might want to freshen a catnip toy by rubbing the herb all over it.

You can also grow your own catnip. Depending on where you live, you might keep a pot outside on a window ledge, have an outdoor herb garden, or, if conditions are right, set a plant inside your house or apartment. Pet supply stores and mail-order catalogs offer starter kits. If you have quite a little outdoor patch going, give some thought to harnessing that power into catnip gifts for friends and their pets.

How Cats Play Together at Home

You can enjoy many games with it, but your cat is still playing with a human. Romping with another feline, however, it plays different games with rules we'll never comprehend. That is one of several good reasons for having two cats. Only with another cat can a cat be, well, a cat.

The two will wrestle, chase each other from room to room, or sit together on a windowsill, facing each other or back to back. If Sidney jumps onto the counter to lick the butter dish, Samantha will watch. Next thing you know, *she's* on the counter licking the butter dish. Cats set both good and bad examples for each other.

Cats being together can be especially important during long days when their owner is at work or away on business or vacation. Even when they're not playing together, the cats will be reassured and comforted by each other's presence. There is the occasional cat who does not *like* its feline housemates, however, and you must respect its preferences.

It's Been Said

"When I play with my cat, who knows whether I do not make her more sport than she makes me?"

—Michel de Montaigne

Everyday Concerns

brush
brush

Everyone knows that cats are survivors. They are, in fact, one of those species that seems to have undergone little or no change over the past 8,000 or more years. So why can't we leave them alone?

Let's look at the question in human terms. Why do we shower, brush our teeth, shave, shampoo, and blow-dry our hair? Certainly the human race could survive without all that (and save some time, too!). Why do we take vitamins? Why do we go on vacation, celebrate important dates, and decorate our homes? Most of us could keep going without that stuff.

The answer? We don't want just *life*, we want a better life. And we want a better life for our feline companions as well. To significantly improve your cat's lifestyle takes only a small human commitment to some of its everyday concerns.

Why Do Cats Need Combs?

Most cats spend almost as much time grooming as Tammy Faye Bakker. Grooming is more than instinct for a cat, it's an art form! So why do we have cat combs, double-sided cat combs, undercoat rakes, slicker brushes, curry brushes, and cat grooming gloves? It all boils down to three human goals:

➤ Optimum health for the cat

➤ Optimum comfort for the humans who share their living quarters with the cat

➤ Beauty

When cats groom themselves by licking their fur, they remove dead hair and debris and aerate their coats. For many shorthaired cats, self-grooming is sufficient for everyday cleanliness so that humans need to step in only occasionally. Longhaired cats, however, need considerably more attention.

Most experts recommend grooming longhaired cats for at least 15 minutes a day to prevent coat tangling and matting. The most common places for mats to form are behind a cat's ears, under the legs, and on the belly. Fine hair in these areas can begin tangling and matting within hours of grooming. Once mats become established, they spread like mold on bread. They become a hiding place for fleas and a breeding area for both bacterial and fungal infections.

A newly formed mat can be carefully separated and un-tangled using a gentle spreading motion of your fingers. A small but somewhat more established mat can be cut out with blunt-nosed scissors. A cat that is severely matted, however, may need to be anesthetized by a veterinarian to have the mats removed surgically. Occasionally, a severely matted cat is shaved by a groomer. The coat will grow in again in three to four months.

From a human comfort point of view, grooming your cat will keep down the amount of shed hair that is deposited on your furniture and clothing. It will also keep down the amount of cat dander in the air, which might allow people with allergies to visit you!

And finally, beauty. If cats are living sculptures, if their movements are music, if their very presence improves the look of a room, then it follows that we humans should groom them to be all they can be, both for them and for ourselves.

Ears, Eyes, Nose, Teeth, and Claws

Most cats do a fine job of keeping their own ears clean. Earwax (a yellow-brown substance often found at the base of a cat's ears) is produced by the cerumen glands and is perfectly normal. If it builds up excessively or if your cat's ears become dirty from its outdoor adventures, you can clean them with cotton balls dipped in warm olive or mineral oil. Do not put cotton swabs down into your cat's ear canals.

Unlike humans, cats do not cry by shedding tears. Excessive tearing usually indicates a medical problem and should be reported to your veterinarian. Sometimes small scraps of debris will collect at the corners of a cat's eyes. These can be gently removed with a moist cotton ball. Some cats of Persian descent with flat faces are prone to tearing and may develop tear stains from their eyes. These can be washed with a moist cotton ball or soft cloth.

A cat's nose is extremely sensitive, generally needs no special care, and should not be tampered with by humans. A runny nose or a particularly dry nose are both signs that something is wrong.

Many cat owners, even the devoted ones, object to the idea of cleaning a cat's teeth. But unattended problems with teeth and gums can cause cat halitosis, which is something you do not want! Cat halitosis produces a horrible, urine-like smell from the mouth. It is a metaphoric red flag telling you that your cat's health has been endangered.

Experts suggest brushing the teeth with a soft child-size toothbrush. You can use plain water or a specially formulated cat toothpaste. *Do not use human toothpaste because some brands contain detergents that could be harmful to cats.*

Some outdoor cats and all indoor cats will need to have their claws clipped from time to time. Twice a month is usually a good routine. Unless your cat is particularly docile, it is generally best to clip only a few claws at a time. If you're just beginning this grooming activity or if you're worried about clipping too much, it's better to err on the conservative side and clip more often.

To clip the claws, press gently on the top of the cat's foot so that the claw comes forward and is exposed. Except when cutting black claws, you will be able to see a pink area called the quick. Cut the nail just up to the quick. Do not cut through the quick because it will bleed and be painful for the cat (see the drawing on the next page). With black claws, you will need to learn by experience approximately where the quick is. Begin conservatively by cutting only the tip of the claw.

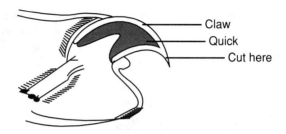

Trim the claw just beyond the quick.

It's Bath Time—or Is It?

Most cats are quite certain that water is intended only for drinking, and they can't understand why any self-respecting animal would want to douse its fur with it. So why should we put them through a bath?

Some cats (notably toms who are allowed outdoors) don't do quite as thorough a job at self-grooming and hygiene as others. Most humans find it more pleasant to have them a little cleaner while they are in the house. Baths are also a means of controlling fleas and are necessary for some skin problems.

Unless your cat was introduced to baths as a kitten, it may object (with various degrees of force and fury) to the idea of being bathed. The bathing procedure, therefore, may require two people at first, one to hold the cat and one to do the washing. Try to talk reassuringly to your cat, keeping it as calm as possible. If the cat objects fiercely, do not hold tighter and force the animal down. This will make an issue out of baths that may never get resolved. Instead, let the cat go and try again later.

When preparing for the bath, place a rubber mat or a cloth bath mat at the bottom of the sink or tub. This will give the cat something to dig its claws into if it should feel the need to hold on. About four inches of water will be

adequate for most baths, but be sure the water is warm
enough. A cat's body temperature is higher than ours, so
the water should feel quite warm to your touch. (About 90
to 95 degrees Fahrenheit is okay.)

Your cat may not like having a bath!

Be especially careful when soaping the cat to avoid its sensitive eyes, ears, and nose. Rinse thoroughly after the
shampoo and then towel dry. Many professional groomers
suggest using a hair dryer set at a low speed to dry the
coat before releasing the cat. Most cats won't object to the
hair dryer.

Tabby Tips

A cat's skin is very sensitive! Be sure to use a shampoo
made for cats. The residues from some human shampoos
could prove toxic to the cat when licked. If you can't get
cat shampoo and the bath *must* be given immediately, use
baby shampoo.

Shedding and the Healthy Coat

Shedding is a normal process for cats. When cats are allowed to go outdoors, a molting or "blowing of coat" usually occurs twice a year (spring and fall). Among indoor cats, shedding is often a more continuous process with some extra emphasis in the spring and fall. Unusually heavy shedding, shedding at unexpected times, or shedding confined to certain areas of the body can all be signs of illness.

The cat's self-grooming during periods of heavier shedding increases the formation of hair balls because more hair is loose and therefore more is ingested. This is a process you want to minimize as much as possible by extra grooming. Even if you don't ordinarily groom your cat, you should make a valiant attempt to do some grooming during shedding season. It will keep your house cleaner and your cat healthier.

Hair Balls

If you see your healthy cat vomiting, don't panic. It's probably a hair ball.

Hair balls occur when ingested hair collects in the stomach. They are normal in cats, but they can sometimes lead to serious obstructions requiring surgery. The best prevention methods are regular grooming, adding some insoluble fiber (grass or rye grass, for example) to the diet, and administering a hair-ball prevention product, such as mineral oil, to the cat. For a choice of products and advice on how much to use, consult your veterinarian. Do not rely on printed product labels.

When a cat coughs up a hair ball, it is usually a brown mass, often tubular, that comes up alone or along with some clear, sometimes foamy fluid. Hair balls are also sometimes evacuated with the stools. Lack of appetite or constipation can be symptoms of a hair ball problem.

About Those Skin Bugs

Fleas, lice, ticks, and mites all attack the skin of the cat. Their bites cause itching, sometimes inflammation and eczema, and sometimes diseases such as Lyme disease and mange. Cat fleas are also intermediary hosts for tapeworms.

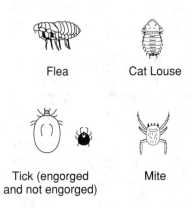

Flea   Cat Louse

Tick (engorged   Mite
and not engorged)

There are many over-the-counter products available to control fleas, lice, and ticks. These include a variety of pills, liquids powders, and shampoos. Most of them work quite well for moderate infestations, but advanced cases will need medical attention. Be careful to choose only products made for cats, because dog products can cause allergic reactions and serious irritations. In some cases, the reactions are so severe that they cause toxicity and even death. Even some flea collars made for cats may cause a skin reaction on some cats, and, in light of the fact that the newer products are more effective and safer, things like collars, powders, and dips are best avoided altogether.

One of the newest products for flea control does not kill fleas. Instead, it sterilizes the fleas that bite your cat so that they cannot reproduce. It is available through your veterinarian. Administered once a month in pill form, this product is most effective on indoor cats who do not bring new fleas into the house. A similar new product is a liquid that you rub on your cat's neck. It absorbs into the skin to kill fleas.

There are several kinds of mites that infest cats and cause different diseases. They are minute, almost invisible, and more difficult to eradicate than fleas or lice. In most cases, you'll need veterinary help.

Engorged ticks, on the other hand, are easily seen and need to be removed from the skin as soon as possible. Wet the head of the tick with alcohol, wait two minutes, and then remove the entire tick by pulling evenly with tweezers.

To guard against an infestation that grows and gets out of hand, be aware of changes in your cat's behavior patterns. Itching and scratching, rubbing the head on the floor (especially the ears), persistent shaking of the head, and agitated restlessness can all indicate a worsening situation with external parasites. If you suspect that the methods you are using are not working adequately, don't put off an appointment with the vet. The longer you wait, the more difficult the cure will be.

What No One Wants to Talk About: Worms

Many cats have worms at some point in their lives. Common symptoms requiring immediate attention are a distended abdomen (pot belly) accompanied by loss of weight, restless and uncomfortable behavior, loss of appetite, and rubbing the anal area on carpets or floors. Tapeworms are usually first seen as small segments that look like grains of rice, except they're crawling under your cat's tail or around the anus. Worms may also be seen in the litter box, or if your cat vomits.

A cat dragging its bottom could have worms.

Cats are susceptible to several kinds of intestinal parasites, including roundworms, tapeworms, hookworms, coccidiae, and trichinellae. It is essential that your veterinarian identify the parasite infestation in order to prescribe the proper medication. You'll need to gather stool samples, sometimes more than once.

Tabby Tips

Don't rely on the over-the-counter products to rid your cat of worms. They are not always effective. A cat with worms needs to see a vet.

To Sleep, Perchance to Dream

Sleep. There are those who say it's what cats do best. Most healthy adult cats sleep away 50 to 60 percent of each day, while some manage 70 percent. Senior cats and very young kittens can get that figure up to 80 percent easily. How do they do it?

In the first place, they have different body rhythms than we do. Cats are naturally nocturnal animals, but they don't stay up all night nor sleep all day. They prefer many short periods of light sleep and a few periods of deep sleep over the human pattern of one long sleep per 24-hour day.

During periods of light sleep, cats are pretty much aware of what's going on around them. In fact, the British say, "The cat sees through shut lids." Cats can either move from light sleep into deep sleep or from light sleep into instant awareness and action.

Like humans, cats have at least two different types of sleep, as measured by brain waves: slow-wave or quiet sleep, and REM (rapid eye movement) sleep. During slow-wave sleep, the cat relaxes its muscles, and brain activity slows to a rhythmic pattern. The cat, however, can be easily awakened and maintains enough muscle tone for it to hold its head up in the sleeping sphinx position if it wants to.

REM sleep is deeper but lasts considerably less time. In humans, it's usually the time during which we dream. Most experts believe that it is also the time that cats dream. Many cat people have seen their "sound asleep" pet suddenly begin to twitch its tail, move its feet, or sometimes even make aggressive sounds. It's probably a dream that would rival a movie chase scene!

It's Been Said

"Cats are *always* elegant."

—John Weitz

Chapter 14

Professional Health Care

In This Chapter

➤ About vets

➤ Weight watching

➤ The importance of spaying and neutering

➤ Common cat diseases

➤ That old cat!

Being a small animal veterinarian is a lot like being a pediatrician. Your patients can't tell you where it hurts, how much it hurts, or when it hurts. Instead, communication and interpretation of the symptoms come from a loving caregiver who is always anxious, who doesn't always trust that you're doing the right thing, who pays the bill, and who doesn't always listen to your advice.

But like it or not, most pet owners admit that the vet knows more than they do—about some things. The vet also has the tools to prevent some diseases and cure many others. About making a cat more comfortable, however…well, maybe that's a joint effort, 50 percent caregiver and 50 percent veterinarian.

How to Select a Vet

Should you simply drive to the vet's office nearest you? Should you check the phone book for names and pick one? It's risky. Having read this far, you certainly know that cats are different from other animals. They have some unusual sensitivities and reactions to chemicals, and they have some instinctual drives that prompt them to hide their infirmities. You need a vet who knows cats well.

Cat people seem to find each other wherever they are, and you should seek them out when you begin vet hunting. Talk with cat owners or cat groomers who have used the veterinarians you are considering. You can also call and ask for the names of cat specialists from a veterinary college near you or from your local animal shelter.

The American Animal Hospital Association in Denver, Colorado, is a national trade association for veterinarians. If you call them at (800) 883-6305 and give them your zip code, they will provide you with a list of member veterinarians in your area. You can even get professional bios on the vets you are considering as well as order a number of health-care pamphlets. If you prefer a referral to a cats-only vet, you can call the American Association of Feline Practitioners at (505) 343-0088.

What to Expect at the Annual Checkup

Most people take their cats to the vet once a year as a preventative measure. A lot can happen in a year in the life of a cat. At an annual physical, the vet should check the cat's body systems and overall health and record the results for future comparison against a time when there might be trouble developing.

Just like a human doctor, your veterinarian will listen to the heart and lungs and palpate the organs in the cat's abdomen. He or she will examine the condition of the ears and check both the ears and skin for external parasites. Teeth and gums are inspected for damage or infection. The veterinarian will also check the eyes and nose for unusual discharges. Anal glands are checked for proper function and to be sure they are not impacted. The vet might need to inspect a stool sample for worms or carry out a routine worming.

Do I Have to Get on the Scale?

What do humans hate most in a doctor's office? The scale! But fat cats are not nearly so self-conscious as fat humans. In fact, they rather like themselves the way they are and will proceed quite happily through life. Studies show that added weight has little effect upon a cat's life span. Hey, maybe we humans should take a cue!

Some cats are naturally lean and some are not. Diet and exercise can help maintain the cat at its optimum weight, but that weight is determined in the genes and cannot be changed much. You just can't change a cuddly, pudgy Persian into a sleek, scintillating Abyssinian. The moral of the story is to love the cat you have.

That does not mean, however, that your cat's weight should not be monitored and charted by the vet. Sudden weight gains or losses are often indicative of disease. Fat cats are more prone to urinary problems than lean cats. They can also injure their joints more easily.

A genuinely overweight cat (this is only about 10 percent of the cat population) can be encouraged to slim down a bit for health and comfort. However, you should put your cat on a reducing diet only with the advice and assistance of your veterinarian because proper nutritional balance is extremely important to success. Never try to reduce your cat's weight with a forced fast. Fasting by overweight cats can bring on fatty liver disease (hepatic lipidosis), which can be fatal.

Oh, No! Shots!

Many serious diseases in cats can now be prevented through immunization. In each of the following diseases, once the initial immunization is established, the adult cat needs only boosters to maintain its immunity. The frequency of required booster shots depends upon the disease and the product used to establish immunity, and has recently been the subject of much debate. Discuss a vaccination schedule with your veterinarian, and don't be afraid to ask questions.

Here is a list of the most common vaccinations:

➤ *Feline distemper:* A very infectious and potentially fatal viral disease that can be spread from cat to cat or brought into the house on human hands and even shoes that have touched an infected cat. Also called feline panleukopenia, feline infectious enteritis, show fever, and cat plague. It is not related to canine distemper.

➤ *Rabies:* A fatal disease that can be transmitted from animals to humans. All cats should be inoculated; many states require it.

➤ *Feline leukemia virus:* Similar in some ways to the human HIV virus, but not exactly the same. It is diagnosed by a blood test and is transmitted from cat to cat by long exposure to saliva or blood, usually while mating. *It cannot be transmitted to humans.* FeLV-negative queens (breeding females) should be inoculated before mating. Pregnant cats should not be inoculated. Many stud cat owners insist that visiting queens be tested before mating.

➤ *Cat flu:* Actually two viruses with similar symptoms
that a combined vaccine usually inoculates against.
The symptoms of both viruses include coughing,
sneezing, and a runny nose and runny eyes. The viruses are a special threat to the very young and the
very old. A cat who has the disease and recovers can
become a carrier.

Two Nasty Viral Diseases

Effective and reliable vaccines have not yet been found for
two life-threatening viral diseases. Experts believe, however, that current work will lead to solutions that will conquer them.

Feline immuno-deficiency virus (FIV) has frightened many
pet owners because it resembles AIDS even more than
FeLV. This virus attacks and breaks down the cat's im-
mune system. It cannot be transmitted to humans, nor
can cats get the HIV virus. Like HIV, however, many cats
infected with FIV enjoy long periods of good health before secondary infections take their lives. It is usually diagnosed by a blood test. If your cat is FIV positive, you
should keep him or her away from other cats.

Feline infectious peritonitis (FIP) can appear in two forms:
wet and dry. Symptoms of the wet form are a swollen abdomen, diarrhea, vomiting, and weight loss. The dry form
affects the central nervous system with symptoms that include jaundice, respiratory problems, loss of coordination,
and, near the end, seizures. FIP was a rare disease but is
becoming more common. When contracted, it is virtually
always fatal. A vaccine has been in use for more than five
years now, but there are still questions surrounding it.

Signs That Your Cat Might Be Sick

Because your cat can't tell you it's sick and will, in fact, often try to hide it from you, you must become aware of the

behavior clues that should signal a vet visit. The following is an alphabetical list of symptoms and behaviors, along with some of the illnesses they might indicate:

➤ *Breathing difficulties:* Foreign bodies, head cold, leukemia, upper respiratory system disorder

➤ *Changes in the skin:* Allergies, external parasites, fungus infection, improper diet

➤ *Constipation:* Blockage of the intestine, foreign bodies, infectious peritonitis, head cold, kidney stones, uterine infection, worms

➤ *Coughing and sneezing:* Cat flu, head cold, upper respiratory system disorder

➤ *Diarrhea:* Hair balls, improper diet, infectious peritonitis, kidney problems, leukemia, poisoning, worms

➤ *Fever:* Bacterial infection, flea infestation, hair balls, kidney problems, upper respiratory system disorder, viral infection

➤ *Increased thirst:* Diabetes, flea infestation, kidney problems, liver disease, leukemia, poisoning, uterine infection

➤ *Runny eyes and nose:* Cat flu, feline pneumonitis, injury, upper respiratory system disorder

➤ *Scratching ears and shaking head:* Ear infection, ear mites

➤ *Swollen body:* Distemper, fleas, foreign bodies, infectious peritonitis, leukemia, worms

➤ *Vomiting:* Foreign bodies, hair balls, improper diet, infectious peritonitis, poisoning, worms

How to Give a Cat a Pill

The incredible resistance and agility of the cat is again demonstrated whenever it takes two people to give an eight-pound animal a pill (and that seems to be more often than not!).

In the two-person method, one person holds the cat while the other pries open the cat's mouth by placing the thumb and forefinger on either side of the jaws and pushing firmly but gently. The pill is popped in as far back on the tongue as possible. The cat's mouth is then shut and held closed while the nostrils are covered with a finger (briefly—the cat has to breathe!). This forces the cat to swallow. Some pet owners also stroke the cat's throat at this time.

Be sure that the cat does swallow. Some wily cats will hide the pill in their mouth and then spit it out when the pill administrator is not looking.

Tabby Tips

Never give your cat aspirin. No, not even baby aspirin! Aspirin is likely to cause hemorrhaging in the cat's gastrointestinal tract. It also depresses bone marrow activity, which makes replacement red blood cells, and it can be harmful to the kidneys. Acetaminophen (Tylenol and other brands) also causes problems, but for other reasons.

If two people are not available, you can get some added restraining power (and protection from claws) by wrapping the cat in a bath towel, leaving only its head showing. Then follow the steps in the two-person method.

Plastic "pill poppers" are also available. They look a little like fat, long syringes. The pill is loaded inside, the cat's mouth is forced open, the popper is placed with the end near the back of the cat's mouth, and the human pushes the plunger. If you choose to use this method, be absolutely certain that the pill popper has a soft tip to prevent injury to the cat's throat. Also, make sure that the pill does not miss its mark or get spit out by the cat.

Some owners try concealing the pill in a favorite treat. Sometimes this works, but sometimes the cat manages to eat all of the treat and then spit out the pill. A more reliable method is to pulverize the pill and mix it with a favorite treat (tuna or liverwurst usually works), then roll up a bite or two, each the size of a nut. If your cat loves butter, you can mix the pulverized pill with a small amount and then put it on your cat's paws. The cat will usually lick it off. Before choosing any of these food-associated methods, however, be sure to check with your vet because some medications lose efficacy when mixed with food.

Alternative Medicine

Human interest in natural healing using clinical nutrition and herbal remedies is growing rapidly with more and more people using these methods to supplement traditional medical care. More humans are also using acupuncture, homeopathy, and chiropractic medicine. What has this got to do with cats? Well, there is a movement among veterinarians to recognize and include these healing methods in their practices.

The American Holistic Veterinary Medical Association (AHVMA) was founded in 1982 and has grown to a membership of more than 500 veterinarians and other health-care practitioners. If you want to include alternative medicine in your cat's care, you can get the names of practitioners near you by sending a self-addressed stamped envelope to AHVMA, 2214 Old Emmorton Rd., Bel Air, MD 21015. You can also ask your veterinarian and local animal protection agencies for referrals.

What Humans Can Catch

Only a few diseases can be transmitted between cats and humans. It is important that you know what they are and how to avoid them:

➤ *Rabies:* Even indoor cats should be immunized, just in case they get out into the world on occasion.

➤ *Fleas:* Cat fleas prefer cats, then dogs. But if there's nothing else, they'll jump on humans.

➤ *Ringworm and other skin fungus:* Cats, especially longhaired varieties, can bring the spores (which are often picked up from the soil around a house) indoors on their coats. Humans can get ringworm by petting the cat or from shed hair in the house, even though the cat does not get the disease. When humans have ringworm, the cat should be treated also, and the house, particularly the carpets, should be cleaned with anti-fungal solution wherever possible.

➤ *Toxoplasmosis:* Toxoplasma is a microscopic parasite that can be ingested by the cat from undercooked or uncooked meat (field prey). It does not usually make the cat ill, but it is passed in the feces. Its danger to humans is primarily to pregnant women because it can cause severe damage to the brain and eyes of the fetus. It is recommended, therefore, that pregnant women do not clean litter boxes. Toddlers and young children should also be kept away.

The Importance of Spaying and Neutering

There are three reasons why spaying or neutering a cat benefits both cats and humans:

➤ Population control

➤ Behavior modification

➤ Improved health

Many people, however, hesitate to spay their female cat or neuter their male cat because they feel it is somehow unkind. But is it kind to allow the queen to bear litter after litter in endless repetition? Is it kind to let the tom roam to fight and fight again until he contracts a fatal disease or is killed by a car? Or is it kinder to remove the sex drive that rules cats' lives, thus allowing them to live fuller and longer lives as human companions? Let's look at the three reasons to spay or neuter.

Population Control

The cat population is increasing around the world, and particularly in North America. This is fine if it means that more and more people are making cats their pet of choice. But there's more to the statistics. The number of feral cats in our cities and our suburban residential areas is also growing rapidly.

Cat Language

Feral cats are descendents of domestic cats that have been born in the wild.

Cats without a home are cats struggling to survive by eating from garbage cans and sleeping in the dug-out areas around basement windows. They fight, they are prone to abscesses and other diseases, they transmit fatal viral diseases from one to another, and they often get hit by cars. Other cats are put to death simply because a home cannot be found.

Municipalities and animal protection agencies are struggling to get the cat population explosion under control. Many cities have programs to capture and euthanize abandoned or feral cats. Animal protection agencies, with the help of volunteer veterinarians and concerned citizens, have organized spay and neuter programs in an effort to cut down on the number of cats being put to death. Many shelters are now spaying or neutering kittens before they are released to homes, because studies have shown that these procedures can be done on kittens as young as six weeks without harm.

Behavior Modification

How does spaying or neutering change the behavior of cats? In females it stops the heat seasons from occurring. The queen no longer vocalizes her need throughout the day and night. Her rubbing, rolling, and posing stops, as well as the spraying that some female cats take up during their seasons. Spayed females no longer feel the need to escape outdoors to find a mate, and they develop a keener interest in and attachment to their owners. Not least important, there are no new kittens twice a year.

Neutering a male cat usually stops his fighting and his roaming, especially if the neutering is done early in his life. In most cases, neutering will also stop the urine spraying that can leave a seemingly permanent scent in your home. The neutered male is less aggressive and more companionable. He is interested in his owner and what is happening in the house, and he likes to play. Neutering does not make him fat, but overfeeding and boredom will.

Improved Health

Spaying reduces the risk of mammary (breast) cancer in female cats, especially if it is done before the first heat. Sexually intact queens have a seven times higher risk of developing mammary tumors. This statistic is especially important because 85 percent of breast tumors in cats are malignant.

Because the uterus is removed in spaying, the procedure also eliminates all the potential diseases of that organ. These include *pyometra* (a pus-filled uterus), *metritis* (an inflammation of the uterus), and *endometritis* (inflammation of the lining of the uterus).

Neutered male cats live longer than their intact brothers because they get into far fewer fights. With fewer fights, they have a lower risk of abscesses and irreparable wounds. They also roam less and are therefore at lower risk for becoming highway fatalities.

Should You Do It?

Yes! Veterinarians and animal protection groups are in total agreement. There are no negatives to the spay and neuter question. Removing the sex drive in cats improves their behavior in your home, makes them more comfortable in their own lives, and helps control the overpopulation problem in your community.

Common Problems of the Older Cat

There have been reports of cats living 30 years, with one claiming the record at 36, but that is very, very unusual. A 12-year-old cat would be paid Social Security benefits, according to our government's current age guidelines (if cats could collect, that is). A 20-year-old cat should have already gotten a Happy Birthday letter from our president, like every American who lives a whole century.

With age comes some changes. Older cats are less adaptable to stress and sudden changes in day-to-day routines than younger animals. As they age, cats are prone to gradual deafness and to develop many of the same diseases that older humans endure, such as diabetes, heart disease, arthritis, kidney disease, tumors, and constipation.

Unlike humans, many older cats develop hyperthyroidism, a condition in which the thyroid gland overproduces. If your cat is eating normally but losing weight, you should check with your veterinarian because this condition is treatable with medication or surgery.

Just like kittens, older cats are sometimes a problem and often a joy. They are usually more affectionate and attentive than their prime-of-life cousins, they sleep a lot, and they like their comfort. But then again, don't we all?

MEOW!

It's Been Said

"He seems the incarnation of everything soft and silky and velvety, without a sharp edge in his composition."

—Hector Munro

Chapter 15

No Bad Cats

In This Chapter

➤ Instincts and mind games

➤ When people get angry at cats

➤ Cats under stress

➤ Depression is a cat disease, too

➤ Yes, there are cat behavior therapists

Behavior problems are by far the most common reason that cats are brought to a veterinarian or a shelter to be euthanized. More than 8 million cats are put to death each year in the United States—and that's not the whole of it. Those statistics recognize only the cats owned by the kinder, gentler people and do not include the millions of cats that are pushed out of car doors into neighborhoods or wooded areas far from their homes.

Cats Will Be Cats

Unlike dogs, who have lost most of their ancestral wolf traits through their long association with humans, cats are still "wild things" in many of their behaviors. Not only are their ancient instincts strong, but the cat as a species does not seem to want to give them up or adapt them to the needs and desires of their human companions.

Many of the so-called problem behaviors of cats are really just cats doing what comes naturally. The real problem is that many humans don't know what is natural for a cat. Such people attribute human thoughts and emotions to a cat's activities.

A young male cat scratches the leg of the brand-new dining room table, for example, and the distraught owner cries out to her husband that the cat was mad at them because they were late coming home and didn't leave out any food. More likely, the cat was declaring that the table was one of his possessions. Because he is a cat, he makes no association between the scratched table leg and the punishment that follows. But he learns that the man who did the punishing can be an enemy.

There's no doubt about it: Cats are loving companions who bring joy, laughter, and comfort to millions of people; but they are cats. If we accept them into our homes, we must understand their drives and motivations and provide acceptable outlets for the resulting behaviors. If we must train them, we must use methods that cats understand, not human rules and human punishment techniques.

I Couldn't Help It, Ma! Honest!

As a primer, let's look at four of the most common types of cat behavior that humans often find objectionable. Each category includes several normal cat activities that make people scream "Bad cat!" Understanding the underlying drives behind these activities may not make them any more pleasant to us, but it may help us provide for acceptable alternative behaviors, take steps to diminish the drive, and accept and love the cat as a cat.

Aggressive Behavior

You are calmly stroking your cat when suddenly its front feet are wrapped around your hand, claws out. Maybe there's even a little bite before your cat jumps from your lap and runs under the couch. What happened? What did you do wrong?

Usually nothing. Experts don't really know why cats suddenly scratch. They do know, however, that some degree of aggression is natural in all cats, probably stemming from their instinctual survival behaviors. Most cats do a good job controlling this behavior indoors. Their bites and scratches are really just "see what I can do" statements.

Some cats, however, take aggression a few steps further indoors. Sometimes, for example, they will dash out from a hiding place, dig their claws into your ankle, and dash away again. This is unacceptable behavior that can become a ritualized daily occurrence if allowed to continue. Your cat must be made to understand that clawing is not a game and that you, the dominant cat in the house, will not allow it. When the cat attacks, stamp your feet hard, clap your hands, and shout "Bad cat!" or something that makes a challenging sound. If you have one handy, squirt the cat with a water gun.

The best prevention of aggressive behavior in a grown cat starts in kittenhood. It's important that you don't encourage biting, scratching, and attack-the-human-hand games with your kitten. Like the human, what the cat learns in childhood usually stays, either consciously or subconsciously, in its mind.

Aggression between cats in a multi-cat household is more difficult to control. Cats have their own social structure, and most experts advise that cat owners let the cats work it out. If the aggression continues longer than a few weeks, if it becomes more than you can tolerate, or if a cat becomes injured, however, step in and then try to find another home for one of the fighting cats.

Beyond the Litter Box

Cats are clean animals and are so easily trained to use a litter box that many people forget that they can, and sometimes do, use other places to relieve themselves. Once a new "place" for a cat to relieve itself is established, the habit may be hard to break. When you come upon the initial deviation, try to find the cause.

When cats deposit feces just outside the litter box, it often means that the box has not been cleaned recently and is too dirty for the cat. Frequently switching from one type or brand of litter to another can also cause some cat to reject their litter box, especially older cats who do not like change. Find a type of litter that you and the cat like, and stick with it.

Frequent urinating outside the litter box is a very common problem. It can be a sign of kidney disease, bladder infection, diabetes, emotional stress, or another disease. Rubbing your cat's nose in the soiled place and spanking, as is often done with dogs, will not have any effect on the cat's behavior. (Incidently, it doesn't have any effect on a dog's behavior, either.) Your first step in correcting this type of behavior is to have the cat checked by a vet to make sure there is no underlying physical cause. Then you must look for the behavioral cause.

Cat spraying (urinating for scent marking) is instinctual behavior used to establish territory, and sometimes this outdoor trait is moved indoors. It might occur when a new cat (or even a new person such as a baby or a new husband, wife, or roommate) is introduced to the household. It might occur when a cat is moved to a new house or apartment. Or it might occur when a cat sees other cats through the window or perhaps hears or smells them outside the apartment door.

While working on this problem and trying to make your cat feel comfortable again, it is often a good idea to make the places your cat has already used as inaccessible as possible. Some cat owners block off such places, others even put the food bowls there. Keeping a cat away from a place that still carries the odor of urine (even if humans can't smell it) will make the formation of a new habit less likely. Some owners also add another litter box in the house, giving the cat a choice of more than one location. (More about spraying in just a bit.)

A tomcat spraying.

Destructive Behavior

Scratching furniture and woodwork is another residual behavior of the instinct of cats in the wild to mark their territories by leaving scratch marks on trees. All kittens will try out their scratch-marking ability, so kittenhood is the time to teach them to use a scratching post. If you bring an adult cat into your house, it may take a bit longer to discourage scratching, but it can usually be done. Spend time each day playing with your cat near the scratching post and encouraging the cat to use it.

Some cats left home alone all day become bored and use territorial scratching as an amusement. It's important, therefore, to have plenty of cat toys about and (many people say) more than one cat, since they do amuse each other once they decide to get along.

Some cats suck on yarn and woolen fabrics, and some even eat holes in their owners' clothes. No one knows exactly why they do this; one theory is that it reminds them of suckling, but that's only a theory. When wool or other fabric is actually eaten, it is usually passed without harm through the cat, but it does sometimes cause digestive problems and even blockages that require surgery. If you notice your cat eating or sucking on wool, it is best to keep all fabrics out of its reach. Siamese and Burmese cats are often wool suckers.

Some cats eat houseplants. Although the cat is primarily a carnivore, most cats like a little salad now and then. Houseplants, therefore, are tempting. Some of them are poisonous, while others just taste good.

What to do? Well, you have three choices. You can avoid battle with your cat by keeping your favorite plants out of reach, you can provide plenty of plants that are edible and tasty for the cat to eat at floor level, or you can opt for silk plants or no plants in your home.

Fear

Fear of humans is instinctual in the tiger. Sometimes a vestige of that instinct appears in the cat. It can be a good thing if it helps your cat recognize you as the dominant being in the household and worthy of due respect. Fear can bring about a behavior problem, however, when a cat will not come out of hiding as long as a stranger is in the house or, worse yet, when a cat hisses, spits, and attacks a stranger. This is a problem that takes both patience and perseverance on the part of the owner and sometimes requires professional help.

Learned fear, such as the fear of getting a shot or a bath, can cause aggressive self-preservation behavior such as scratching, biting, or trying to escape, but it can often be calmed with patient handling. If your cat shows aggressive fear, proceed very slowly or, if possible, put the activity aside for another time.

Tabby Tips

What does it mean when your cat starts racing about the room like a dervish? Is it afraid? Has it gone temporarily mad? Hardly. Such behavior is perfectly normal for the cat. Most experts believe it is a release of tension. It occurs most often near sunset—the cat's natural hunting time. Don't worry. It's unlikely the cat will bash into a wall, and it will be its own normal self in just a few minutes.

Mind Games

Despite the many written testimonials on the similarity of the cat mind and the human mind, there is still a great deal of mystery about the cat. We don't always know why cats do what they do. We do know, however, that it is usually nonproductive and sometimes actually destructive to attribute human motivations to cat activities.

He Did It for Spite

One woman was trying to complete the knitting of a baby afghan while her son, his wife, and their new baby were visiting. When Clarance the cat curled up next to her (on top of the already finished portion of the afghan) she shooed him away briskly. That evening, the whole family went out to dinner. When they returned home, Clarance had pulled the afghan out of the knitting bag, pulled the circular needle out of the work, and unraveled and tangled several inches of the intricate pattern.

The poor grandmother was bombarded with conflicting emotions: "He did it for spite! He was jealous of the baby! He wanted more attention!" she cried as she scooped up Clarance and pushed him down the cellar stairs.

What really happened? Maybe Clarance liked the feel of the soft wool and was trying to make a comfortable bed for himself. Maybe he was fascinated with the regular movement of the knitting needles and wanted to play with them. Who knows? However, the human emotion of spite was probably *not* the motivator.

She Manipulates Us Horridly

"Jezebel gets what she wants, one way or another," says a Kansas man. "If I'm trying to read the newspaper, she'll rub around my legs, walk over my shoulders, bat the newspaper with her claws—whatever it takes to make me stop and do what *she* wants to do. She's better at getting attention than most of the humans I know!"

Getting human attention seems to be a natural talent of most household cats, but some subtle creatures seem to go even further and try to manipulate human behavior. Faked injuries are commonly reported. For example, a couple who frequently travel noticed their cat limping badly and holding up a front paw as they were packing their suitcases. With nonrefundable flight tickets in hand, they called a relative, who agreed to take the cat to the vet. Nothing could be found despite almost $200 in bills for X-rays, testing, boarding, and observation. The cat was fine when the couple returned home. Two months later when packing for another trip, the limp developed again. But this time, it was the other leg!

Certainly, some of the joy of living with a cat is the intimate contact with a mind that thinks. Cats are neither leaders nor followers, but very independent beings. They are always something of a puzzle and something of a challenge. Maybe that's why we love them so much.

Raging Hormones

Many of the cat behaviors that humans find undesirable, such as scratching and indoor spraying, are greatly intensified by sex-related hormones. Even though he is never allowed outdoors, a tomcat will become agitated when there is a female in season in the neighborhood. He will also react intensely (by spraying, scratching, and sometimes displaying bad temper) if he sees another cat through the window.

Outdoor toms are also usually the culprits in the objectionable caterwauling that occurs during the night. These cries and the frequent fights among toms are usually related to territorial disputes (as are most human wars).

Females are not quite as territorial as male cats, but they too will fight to keep out an unwanted visitor, and they will also mark their possessions. Females in season want to go out looking for a mate, and a female cat will stay in season until she finds one or the weather turns colder. Owners often report personality changes that include impatience, restlessness, and verbal complaining.

For those people who don't want to handle hormone-intensified cat behaviors, there is really only one option:

spaying or neutering all of the cats in the household. No
amount of training will help. These behaviors are stimu-
lated by sexual hormones that create the drives necessary
for procreation and the preservation of the species. These
drives are just as intense as the drives to eat, drink, and
sleep.

When Your Cat Makes You Angry

It would be a rare couple and a rare family that never had
a fight. And it would be a rare cat that never made its
owner angry. But for families and for cats, research shows
that physical punishment and abuse do not work.

If your cat makes you angry, express your anger with
shouts or by punching a pillow. After you cool down, try
to understand the cause of the behavior that made you
angry. Then try to think of a way to prevent it, preferably
something that makes the act undesirable to the cat.

Let's say, for example, that you leave your Thanksgiving
turkey on the countertop to cool a bit before carving and
go into the living room to join your guests for some hors
d'oeuvres. While you are there, Henry VIII jumps up on
the counter and begins his feast. Don't throw Henry
against the wall when you discover him calmly washing
his face. In his mind, the turkey was left there just for
him.

Instead, try to make him understand (ahead of time, of
course) that jumping up to the countertop is always un-
pleasant. One man put double-sided carpet tape on the
counters. His cats did not like getting their feet stuck. Because cats are intelligent and don't repeat behaviors that
cause them discomfort, it took only a few days to train
them not to jump up.

Cats Under Stress

Many of life's stressful situations for humans are also stressors for cats. Like humans, cats usually respond to stress with changes in their behavior patterns. Some common changes are over-eating or under-eating, over-grooming to the point of licking a spot to baldness, restlessness, and not using the litter box.

Among the most common cat stressors are:

➤ Extended absence of a loved family member

➤ Introduction of a new human into the household

➤ Introduction of a new cat into the household

➤ Long hours of being left home alone

➤ Human stress that changes the behavior of a loved human

➤ Moving to a new home

➤ Loss of a companion cat in the household

Depression Is Real

Some cats, like some humans, suffer from depression, but the cat can't declare, "I'm depressed." It's almost eerie that common symptoms of cat depression are so similar to the symptoms of human clinical depression:

➤ Listlessness

➤ A lack of interest in life

➤ Ungroomed, uncared-for appearance

➤ Changes in eating habits—either refusing food or displaying binge behavior

➤ Changes in sleep patterns

➤ Personality changes

Before assuming that your cat is depressed, it's essential that you take it to the vet for a complete examination. Many of these symptoms can also be caused by a physical illness, such as an infection. If nothing shows up in the exam or the tests, you should try giving the depressed cat extra attention. Besides playing and petting, this includes the grooming that the cat is not doing and perhaps some tempting food if anorexia is a symptom.

Most cats come out of depression with a little help from their humans. But if the condition persists, there are cat-sized doses of anti-depressant drugs available from veterinarians.

Animal Behavior Therapists

There are efforts under way within the American Veterinary Medical Association to make animal behavior therapy a specialty, but there are still few course programs available in veterinary colleges. Some veterinarians have pursued study on their own; others have sought out individuals who work successfully with cats and other animals to refer their patients to.

Some veterinary colleges do have behavior advisors associated with their clinics. Often, they have help lines you can call for advice by phone. There are fees that vary, however, so ask how much it will cost before you start talking.

There has also been some effort made to establish requirements for certification in animal behavior therapy, but to date there are no license requirements anywhere in the United States. That's right: Anyone who thinks they understand animals can hang out a shingle that reads "Animal Behavior Therapist."

The lack of licensing standards, however, does not mean that a person without formal education cannot be a good, or even an excellent, cat therapist. Trying to understand the behavior of an animal that does not speak our language and trying to help that animal and its human owner adapt to life together takes love and tremendous patience. We must remember that we cannot get into the cat's mind because we are not cats.

It's Been Said

"In a cat's eyes, all things belong to cats."

—English proverb

The Unspoken Language of Cats

	Eyes	Ears	Tail	Whiskers
Affection, trust	Wide, pupils normal, slow blinks	Up, forward, and turned slightly to the side	Vertical and cocked slightly over the back	Pointed forward and down
Need, discomfort	Varies with the situation	Usually up and forward, but can vary with the situation	Usually low	Usually up and forward, but varies with the situation
Fear, defense	Very wide, pupils very dilated	Horizontal and to the sides of the head	Fluffed out, swishing from side to side or tucked under	Forward, up, and spread out
Hunting, stalking	Wide, focused, unblinking	Up, pointing forward	Low and still, except for twitches at the end	Forward and tense
Aggression	Narrow, with pupils focused	Laid back against head	Wide sweeps from side to side, sometimes fluffed out and still	Forward and up

Astrological Sun Signs of the Cat

Aquarius (January 21–February 19) Aquarius cats are unpredictable, and that's how they like it! Just when you think they're your best friends, they become remote and detached, looking down at you from a distant perspective. Independence and individuality are their watchwords. With a strange electricity in their nature, they may appear downright flaky at times, and they often can't resist upsetting the status quo—just because. Yet the Aquarius cat is friendly and generally tolerant of your foibles.

Pisces (February 20–March 20) A sweet and dreamy cat who finds it easy to make-believe. The Pisces cat can spend a lot of time entertaining both itself and you with imaginary scenarios. Deeply sensitive both physically and emotionally, their hearts yearn for total oneness with you (on their own terms, of course). Their taste usually runs to seafood, and a little water is not likely to bother them. Be aware of what you are feeling when you're with a Pisces cat, because they tend to absorb your moods.

Aries (March 21–April 20) A real swashbuckler of a cat with a lot of energy, drive, and daring. Aries cats love being where the action is and will not back away from a fight. With a strong sense of self and a me-first attitude, they hate standing on the sidelines and will try to dominate others around them. Spontaneous and impatient, they are first at the food dish.

Taurus (April 21–May 21) A cat who loves the good things in life—a soft cushion, a special place of its own, and gourmet dinners. Laid-back, adagio, and very sensual,

Taurus cats choose food, stroking, and massage. So much good stuff, however, could lead to, well, pudge. Taurus cats are possessive of the things they love, and they can be stubborn. Once habits are acquired, they're hard to break.

Gemini (May 22–June 21)   A curious and playful cat who doesn't want to miss a trick. Gemini cats are alert, clever, and interested in everything. Variety is the spice of their lives; they choose a little of this and a little of that— but not too much of one thing. They are great communicators and enjoy talking (or talking back) to whoever is around. Concentration is not their strong point.

Cancer (June 22–July 23)   The homebody of the cat world. Cancer cats love the security of a warm hearth (or a warm bed). They are sensitive and can be somewhat shy and moody, but they will purr with pleasure at a little TLC. Queens make good mothers, and toms like to be mothered. They love the night, and, in their own quiet way, they are very tenacious about getting what they want.

Leo (July 24–August 22)   Truly the cat who would be king. The Leo cat is proud, regal, and dramatic. Leos like center stage and usually get it. They love flattery and having a fuss made over them. Their vanity, however, will not tolerate belittling, and if you make fun of them, they might go off to seek an appreciative audience elsewhere. But given their royal due, they will be the happiest and most loving of cats—and lord it over you with great aplomb.

Virgo (August 23–September 23)   A very intelligent and discriminating aristocrat. Virgo cats demand only the best and look down upon anything or anyone who is less than perfect. They keep themselves neat and clean and expect their environments to be kept the same way. Virgos have a sense of what seems right and can become nervous if things are not just so. If you win the approval of this cat, you've been bestowed the greatest of compliments.

Libra (September 24–October 23) Unhappy alone, a good friend to all. Cats born in Libra need interaction with others—felines, humans, or even Fido. They have a refined nature and a love of peace and harmony. Too much discord and loud noise can cause nervousness and misery. Libra cats often have trouble making up their minds, like whether or not to go out while you stand there with the door open. But they are so charming and attractive that most humans are happy to be a part of their lives.

Scorpio (October 24–November 22) The animal of sensuous magnetism. The Scorpio cat is intense, passionate, and mysterious. Scorpios have strong desires and expect to get what they want. They will size up a situation instantly, and they can seduce you into doing whatever they want and have you think it was your idea. In fact, they are such experts that you will enjoy being manipulated. But don't cross swords with them—you are sure to lose!

Sagittarius (November 23–December 21) A live wire with a yen for adventure. Sagittarius cats are always ready to explore what's just around the corner or go out to conquer a new world. Very athletic, they will delight you with acrobatic feats and yowl loudly if their needs for exercise and activity are not met. Yet as they get older, they will develop a philosophical bent and prefer to sit on the front porch and contemplate their very full lives.

Capricorn (December 22–January 20) The status-seeker. The Capricorn cat wants to climb to the top—so watch out for your curtains and look for these cats as close to the ceiling as they can get. Capricorns are serious, cautious, deliberate, and determined, and they work hard at whatever they do—even playing! Somewhat insecure, they thrive in a positive environment and appreciate warmth and attention, although they usually won't admit it.

Provided by Julie Leiter, a member of National Council for Geocosmic Research, Inc., and Astrological Society of Princeton.

Index